"My friend Nam Joon Kim is a leading ___ yond. A Korean best-seller, this provocative book is finally available in English. I never knew how much Proverbs focused on laziness and self-love before reading this book. This is a very needed challenge to us all in this age of comfort and affluence."

—MICHAEL HORTON, J. Gresham Machen Professor of Systematic Theology and Apologetics, Westminster Seminary California

Honest and confronting, Rev. Kim unmasks laziness as a virus increasingly infecting Christianity. Yet, combining his pastoral and his scholarly qualities, Kim describes this virus in such a way that every reader will start fighting it long before he or she has finished reading this great book. I can only say with the words of Kim's hero Augustine: take and read. And I would add: do so now.

—HERMAN SELDERHUIS, President, Theological University of Apeldoorn, Director of Refo500

"A church planter, professor, and, most of all, a faithful pastor, Nam Joon Kim is widely known and dearly beloved in Korea. The author of more than 50 books, he is oftentimes called the John Piper of Korea for his love of Jonathan Edwards, the Puritans, and much of the rest of the history of Christianity as well. This book is one of his best. In his typically godly manner, Kim exhorts us in these wonderful meditations on the Proverbs to shun laziness and spend our lives joyfully for God. This is a lesson Pastor Kim himself learned through ardent struggle, and develops with humility. It is a lesson, I hasten to add, that needs to be heeded very closely in the English-speaking world. I am eager to commend it whole-heartedly to you. I pray that God will use this book to wean your affections from the comforts of this world (as the Puritans used to say) and inspire you to diligence for Christ and his kingdom."

—Douglas A. Sweeney, Trinity Evangelical Divinity School

"In these days when self-indulgence is seen as a virtue, my good friend Dr. Nam Joon Kim shows us that the true way to honor and joy is diligently obeying God's will for God's glory. His practical meditations on Proverbs expose the ugliness of the sluggard. They also unveil how busy people may be surprisingly lazy in the things that matter most. A much-needed book for our day!"

—Dr. Joel R. Beeke, President, Puritan Reformed Theological Seminary, Grand Rapids, MI

One of the chief privileges of God's people being international is to hear his Word taught with insights from cultures different from our own—and it is vitally important for our spiritual health that we listen. In recent years I've come to know and hugely admire Nam Joon Kim, a delightfully gentle, generous and godly man, and a truly remarkable Bible scholar who is deeply learned in Puritan reflections upon the Christian life. In Asia he is already regarded as a spiritual giant among Reformed Evangelicals but is relatively unknown in the West. So I am absolutely delighted that this wonderfully insightful reflection upon lessons from Proverbs about laziness is to be made available in English. I have massively enjoyed reading it, for it is peppered with fresh and memorable insights. At a time when many Western authors encourage us to rest sensibly, Nam Joon Kim brings us God's wisdom for how to repent of worldly laziness and work passionately for the glory of God. I thoroughly recommend it!

—RICHARD COEKIN, Director of the Co Mission
church-planting network in London, Senior Pastor
of Dundonald Church, Raynes Park, London

BUSY FOR SELF, LAZY FOR GOD

BUSY FOR SELF
LAZY FOR GOD

Meditations on Proverbs
for Diligent Living

NAM JOON KIM

Translated by Charles Kim & Pierce T. Hibbs
With an introduction by Peter A. Lillback

WESTMINSTER
SEMINARY PRESS

CONTENTS

FOREWORD

The Rev. Nam Joon Kim is an extraordinary pastoral and theological leader from Seoul, South Korea. It has been my privilege to have fellowshipped with him not only at Yullin Church in Seoul where he ministers, but also to have traveled with him in Europe for educational and lecturing opportunities. I am grateful for Rev. Kim for his earnest interest and engagement with the legacy and vision of Westminster Seminary.

Rev. Kim traces his theological roots back through his professors in Korea to a Westminster student who was taught by founding Professor John Murray. Nam Joon Kim is a Westminster man by legacy, friendship, and theological affinity. If there is any doubt about that, one has only to visit his theological library, one of the finest pastor's libraries I have ever seen.

As our friendship has grown, it has become clear to me that Rev. Nam Joon Kim is not a man who is busy for self and lazy for God! His ministry includes family life, pastoring, teaching, itinerate ministry, as well as writing and publishing a host of books and articles. In other words, his life and commitments are precisely of the nature that allow him to write such a pointed and strategic book that aims at the slothful hearts and minds of so many in our postmodern world. In this study, he explores the ancient teachings of the book of Proverbs that address laziness and diligence, emphasizing how devotion to God can be lost in the busyness of life requiring that God's people reestablish energetic priorities pleasing to the Lord.

I heartily recommend this book to readers in the English-speaking world. I do so not only because of my deep respect for the author and his ministry, but also because this book is already a substantial bestseller in Korea and in the Chinese speaking world. Thus, it is an honor to have *Busy for Self, Lazy for God* translated into English through the work of Westminster Seminary and published by Westminster Seminary Press. It is my hope that his study will be celebrated in the English-speaking context as it has been in the Korean and Mandarin languages.

Please read this book knowing that the Holy Spirit through His Word seeks to equip us to be earnest in our service to the Lord. The wisdom of the ancient Scriptures calls on us to engage our daily lives eagerly to the glory God. My prayer is that these faithful reflections by the busy pastor, the Rev. Nam Joon Kim, will encourage you to strive to live your life to the glory of God and thereby enjoy Him both now and forever.

Sincerely in Christ's service,
Dr. Peter A. Lillback,
President, Westminster Theological Seminary, Philadelphia

PREFACE TO THE SECOND EDITION

I could never have imagined that this book, the fruit of very intense personal wrestling and reflection, would have been received so well in such a short amount of time. As one lives out the days of his life ordained for him, there are three things that he should consider to make his remaining time effective and productive: (1) he must pour his time into critical matters rather than into trivialities; (2) he must seek out ways to become more competent and skilled in his calling; and (3) he must make every effort to live diligently not for himself but for God. This is because, in the context of human depravity, one is diligent in achieving his self-centered desires while he is lazy in completing and fulfilling his God-given duties. That is why one cannot break free from laziness without a spiritual transformation.

The reason for the release of this revised edition in such a short amount of time was in response to the overwhelming demand of many readers who desired a more popular version that could be taken and read anywhere. During the preparation of this revised edition, I made some small updates on the contents of the later portions of the book. I pray that this book may be used in a way that is truly beneficial for those who desire to live a holy life.

A servant of Christ,
Nam Joon Kim
November 10, 2003

Introduction

The person who has loved me the most in my lifetime has been my late grandmother. My parents' business was in a rural area, while I started elementary school in the metropolitan city of Seoul. So, from the moment that I began school until the moment I married and started my own family, my grandmother was the one with whom I spent the majority of my time; she basically raised me. As I was growing up, the one thing my grandmother mentioned more than anything else was my laziness. Whether I woke up a little later or was passing the time doing nothing, she would always remark, "How do you expect to accomplish anything later on if you're this lazy right now?"

I came to realize how dangerous laziness is when my relationship with God became deeper and more intimate, and when I truly yearned to live for his glory. Although I knew that I was saved and God had adorned me with his unconditional love, it was not until later that I came to see how limited and short our lives on earth really are, and even if one has a burning desire to live for God's glory, that desire will never spread unless sufficient time is given to develop it. Also, I began to understand that laziness is not a simple issue to deal with, but is a very complex issue because the root rotting one's soul is self-love, and self-love is complex matter, reaching into every corner of our lives. Another thing that made things more difficult for me was that it seemed that my lazy nature could at any time rear its ugly head and make the struggle and fight to become more holy even more difficult.

After experiencing revival in my life, I began to abhor laziness. However, I was frequently reminded of its presence in me, as the new man in me would fight with the old man constantly. As I continued to hate laziness, I made sure to give life my all every day and tell myself that this is not my day or time, but God's, which also forced me to become better and wiser at using my time. However, I can still see remnants of laziness lurking inside me. I hate this about myself, but I am certain that God hates it even more than I do. He loves *me* unconditionally, but he does not love *my laziness*.

There were many times when I was exhausted because of the internal struggle I had with laziness, but thinking about the life of Jesus brought great comfort and strength, and straightened me out whenever I was sick and tired of putting up a fight to live diligently. When we consider the life of Jesus, it amazes me how he never had a place to lay down his head, and how he completely devoted himself to his mission; laziness and Christ's life were clearly worlds apart. What's more, I consider his life to have been a liquid one. What I mean is that Jesus shed his blood, sweat, and tears for us. He poured himself out. That is what we must strive for.

We must have the same heart and attitude that George Whitefield had, who once exclaimed, "I had rather wear out than rust out."[1] We must be willing to deny ourselves and take up our crosses daily (Matt 16:24; Mark 8:34; Luke 9:23). We must model our lives on the liquid life of Christ.

This book is an attempt to introduce in words a portion of my epiphany on how laziness is a secret and great enemy that stands in the way of the Christian pursuit of holiness. Although many Christians are willing to sacrifice much and take ownership of their sanctification, unfortunately very few realize how great an enemy laziness is. This causes much failure and heartbreak, which is the reason why I wrote this book. Rather than being a sweet and delightful treat for your soul, this will more likely be akin to a very bitter spoonful of medicine, like it was for me a long time ago when I also tasted it. Nonetheless, as you read this book, I urge you to join me and many followers of Christ in becoming a diligent seeker of truth, one who faithfully follows Jesus. May this book enrich, enlighten, convict, and challenge you to become a more holy follower of our Lord.

A servant of Christ,
Nam Joon Kim
August 7, 2003

---

1   Arnold A. Dallimore, *George Whitefield: The Life and Times of the Great Evangelist of the Eighteenth-Century Revival*, vol. 2 (Edinburgh: The Banner of Truth Trust, 1995), 505.

PART I:

To Those Very Familiar and Intimate with Laziness

1

Laziness and the Christian Life

Sinful Remnants of Lethargy

It is a strange truth that spiritual travesty can bring us to grin when we should grieve. Some years ago, after preaching in a church that had been planted in a developing city, I enjoyed a meal with my hosts. As we ate, we shared our thoughts about the gospel and discussed, among other things, how it seems that the majority of Korean churches no longer preach the good news—the true, life-altering gospel of Christ. Nor do they facilitate its accompanying spiritual transformation in the lives of believers. At one point in our discussion, one of the hosts said, "Reverend Kim, even though Korean pastors preach the gospel from the pulpit, and reinforce its importance in the pews, when we visit church members and see how they live, it seems the gospel isn't worth a penny to them." At this, everyone at the table burst into laughter.

But then the laughter tapered off into silence, and the mood went from merry to melancholy.

How can a believer overlook the riches of the gospel? How can a Christian's life not be bursting at the seams with spiritual joy? Perhaps it is because he does not make the effort to become more holy. This may seem like an odd conclusion to draw, but joy and holiness are not distant relations; they are brothers, at least for Christians. A life of holiness is a life of joy, and vice versa. Holiness never increases to our detriment; lasting joy never comes at the cost of sanctification. The two go hand in hand.

Now, perhaps we miss the family resemblance between joy and holiness not because it is difficult to see, but because we do not *want* to see it. We are far more comfortable forgetting that Christ did not come into this world—he did not sweat, suffer, and die for our redemption—only to see us maintain the status quo of our spiritual languor. He came to give us life to the fullest (John 10:10). But such life is a cruciform life (Luke 9:23), a life built upon our Spirit-empowered, grace-infused efforts to become more like Christ and to lose our very lives for his sake (Luke 9:24). This does not necessarily mean martyrdom, but it does mean the death of the old, sinful self, a self that was too often guilty of spiritual laziness.

Because we have been redeemed, that old, sinful self has been crucified with Christ. By the devil's schemes we had been held in bondage to sin and death, but now we are set free. We are declared righteous before the Judge of all. What's more, we have become his children through adoption (Eph 1:5). So, after all that he has given for us—after the blood he shed in order to bring us into his holy bloodline—why would we conclude that we are now free to do whatever we want? Does that sound like the response of a person just saved from an eternity of isolation? Certainly not. Yet perhaps it is helpful to remember here that we are not so different from the prodigal son, who came back from his wild ventures and fell down before his father. The happy homecoming of the prodigal did not mean that his body would not be affected by the consequences of his previous lifestyle. Likewise, our old selves are still affecting our new, regenerated selves. We are still shaking free of the prodigal's servile chains, even as we are united to the Prophet, Priest, and King of creation.

It is in light of this union that we trust completely in the triune God of the Bible, harkening to his every word in Scripture, experiencing the grace of the Holy Spirit. Such grace works in us to conform us to the image of God's sinless Son, to burn away the dross of indwelling iniquity so that we might better resemble the purity of Christ. This work of the Spirit is what transforms us—our character, our personality, our life—so that our souls, which once sought to smother the flame of the truth, can let the Spirit's breath ignite it in our daily lives. The flame God kindles in us is our newfound, Christlike identity. And nothing—not even time itself and the pervasive corruption of the world—can snuff it out. In Christ, our holy identity burns in eternity.

But the mere fact that our identity cannot be threatened does not mean that laziness is a fitting response to our God-given holiness. In fact, laziness is itself spiritual impurity, part of the dross of sin that should be burned up. If we do not make an effort, by and through the Spirit, to identify and destroy the root of laziness, then our flame, our Christ-conforming identity, will only dwindle. If we are not daily diligent in understanding God's Word and in *living it out*, we cannot expect to grow spiritually. And plenty of biblical examples confirm this for us, as do men and women in church history. No one who is deeply respected for having extraordinary faith earned such respect through laziness. God always worked through such people, and they took every opportunity to work for God.

Work before Sin, in Sin, and after Sin

Even before we consider great heroes in Scripture who labored diligently in the faith, we should remind ourselves that work was always a part of humanity, even before sin fractured our relationships and corrupted creation. The calling of Adam and Eve was to serve God through their work. They were instructed, as stewards of God's creation and inhabitants of the garden of Eden, "to work and keep it" (Gen 2:15). Such work was a testament to the quieter growth and vivacity that surrounded them. From seeds came saplings, infant trees, which then matured and bore fruit (Gen 2:9). Rivers rushed through the garden (Gen 2:10–14), carrying the riches of life to the surrounding plants and animals. And, on the basis of the curses later pronounced in 3:17–19, we know that beneath them, the soil was home for roots and organic life, supporting everything that grew. In short, all creation, spoken into being by the triune God, worked symbiotically and diligently to maintain the good order of God's world. Adam and Eve, however, held a special place as stewards.

In light of what Genesis 2–3 reveals about work, we must begin our discussion of diligence by remembering that work is a God-ordained, and hence God-honoring, endeavor. People today might think that work is a result of the fall. Had sin not entered our reality (we might think), we could all relax, rolling over on the grass beds that God breathed into being. This is far from the truth. Work is actually a blessing from God. In fact, it is a call to participate in what God has made, a call to image God as the one who always works for our good.

The negative associations we have of work come from the toil and uncertainty of fruitfulness that was brought about by sin.

Now, if what we said earlier is true, if joy and holiness go hand in hand as members of the same family, then we know that Adam and Eve's joy before the fall was complemented by holiness: diligent and attentive work. This complementation follows us even after the fall. If laboring is truly God's blessing and brings abundant joy, then our work today is still a blessing that can—with our obedience to God's Word (which is a result of his saving grace)—bring us spiritual joy.

And the story does not end there. When we who have been brought into Christ by the power of the Spirit are finally finished with our earthly pilgrimage, we will have eternal communion with God. But that communion is not characterized by idleness and boredom; there will, in fact, be heavenly labor to carry out—labor that somehow glorifies God and reflects our sinless, loving relationship with him. For all eternity, the church, God's people, will be gladly serving him with endless praise. We do not know exactly what sort of work God has for us aside from the joy of worship, but we can be sure that it will be "good," just as his original work for us was "good" (Gen 1:31).

Working in a Sin-Stained World

For the present, however, we are still on this side of paradise. As Christians, we still carry around with us our old self (Rom 6:6), who has been crucified with Christ but remains cloistered in darker corners of our lives. So, while the new self makes a Spirit-wrought effort to love and serve the Lord, the old self tries to make us spiritually lazy. We turn a deaf ear toward God's commandments, and our minds no longer swim against the strong current of secular love. And, once we stop swimming against that current, once we feel the subtle ease of nonresistance, then our desire is no longer to obey God; rather, it is to obey the old, sinful self.

Such desires breed laziness, though its growth is hard to recognize. Indeed, our laziness is often hidden from us, which makes it all the more difficult to account for and defend against. But make no mistake: its subtlety means that it is more of an evil, not less of one. The insidiousness of lethargy marks it as one of Satan's allies, a rogue servant of the coy snake. And so when God, as he always does in Scripture, distinguishes between a good nature and an evil nature, laziness is unequivocally grouped with the latter (Matt 25:21, 23, 26).

Just as many do not know the gravity and danger of sin, which stymies our every effort to be more holy, so we often do not consider the perils of lethargy—even when they are revealed to us. Our indwelling sin blinds us to them, as our old self tries to come back from the dead and unite himself with us. Laziness is a part of that unholy effort, and if we become comfortable with it, then seeing it as a serious problem becomes impossible. We can forget that our soul is at stake: two parties have made a claim on it: Satan and the triune God of Scripture. As Christians, we know that only God's claim will hold, but for that very reason we must diligently guard against Satan's attempts to take what does not belong to him.

Starting right now, you and I will begin exploring the subtle sin of laziness as something that prevents us from living a holy life. We will see what we need to do to guard God's claim on our souls, and, as a result, we will discover the dark inner workings of laziness and how it reaches into our hearts and shows itself in our personalities. With the light of the Word as our guide, we will begin to see how ugly laziness is, how appalled we should be that it still haunts us. Then, when we have seen it for what it truly is, we will no longer be drawn to it. We will still have to face the painful reality of its existence in our lives, of course. But, like a cancer patient who has surgery to remove a tumor and then becomes disgusted when he sees it taken from his body, we will be ready to undergo spiritual surgery to have God himself cut out this deadly disease from our souls. Then we can continue to live a holy life before him, to our joy, and for his glory.

Laziness Leads to Heartache

I would like to begin our exploration with my own context as a pastor and church leader in South Korea.

Whenever I think about my country, my heart swells in pain

for one reason: many Korean people are not really faithful; that is, they lack integrity and can often be dishonest, which has a bearing on the financial growth of the country, many times stunting that growth. In all of human history, the world has never seen a country's national income per capita (GNI) increase to $10,000 in such a short amount of time as it did for South Korea. Currently, the GNI for developed countries is $30,000; South Korea is not there yet, but as the country continues to advance technologically and economically, I think it is possible South Korea will reach that milestone in the near future. This may sound like good news, but we must always keep a close eye on *how* such figures are attained by an unfaithful country—by honest means or by deceitful and manipulative means. The former portend economic stability; the latter, economic precariousness. If we ever hope to see this figure rise in a stable way, we cannot continue to live unfaithfully.

In fact, I do not think it is impossible for the GNI per capita to exceed $30,000. But if that is our desire, we must reform our thought and wake up to what is going on around us. Just look at the prevalence of dishonesty these days—particularly in real estate agents, for example. When South Korean real estate agents earn more than a million dollars and yet pay little in taxes, how can anyone expect integrity and a holy life? Integrity—being who you say you are—and holiness—being who God says you should be—are built upon the foundation of trust in God. If that foundation is replaced by materialism and greed, then integrity and holiness are distorted, if not destroyed. Integrity becomes a façade to get you the sinful things in your heart, and holiness becomes measured by the standards of the old sinful self. Rather than being who God says we should be, we are driven to be who we say we want to be.

Too many people in Korea have fallen prey to this destitute way of life. Their lives are not characterized by faithfulness and integrity. That is why, when the 1997 Asian Financial Crisis occurred, although it was painful, I was somewhat thankful to God. Through such difficulties, many Korean citizens were awakened to the heartache that materialism offers, and they were deeply humbled. Some, by God's grace, even changed the way they thought about money and prosperity.

But a problem still remains, since Korean people, like everyone else, tend to forget things, which is both a strength and a weakness. It is a strength in the sense that Koreans can move beyond social and spiritual ills of the past. It is a weakness in the sense that sometimes those ills are useful reminders of how not to act in the future. But we tend to forget the past to our detriment, and this is all the more obvious when looking at Korean history, which twists and snakes through time like a great river. And because there are so many turns, it becomes difficult for us to even reconstruct, let alone change, the nation's historical path. And if we cannot reconstruct or change it, then it seems near impossible to gather what needs to be remembered, and to throw by the wayside what is better off forgotten.

Yet we must try to do so, or the current of the past will flow unchallenged, and we will continue drifting in the present on whatever course was set by our forebears. Only those who live their lives following the right principles can make new waves on the river and disturb the current. As this disturbance grows, it will unbalance others who have been drifting in the current, helping them to become more aware of their surroundings so that they can change. Change will only come about with great waves on the water.

The Witness of the Church

But who can live a life that makes such waves? Who can send ripples across a river that seems bent on its own course? Contrary to our expectations, this is not something that a prominent politician or philosopher can do, for such people are caught in the same current with everyone else. Only Christians, who should be wading *against* the current, can make the change. Only Christians who have endured much pain and have endlessly striven to live a holy life can live out their hope in faithfulness—a hope that counters the illusions of the world and sends ripples to meet the current of sloth. Therefore, I believe that our only option is to fix our eyes on the church.

Both spiritually and historically, the church needs to be its own river, a river pure and clean—the river of life (Rev 22:1)—that rushes to meet and drive back the murky river of the world, a river of lethargy. But this battle of rivers cannot be fought by one or two people; the whole body of Christ must have a hand in this, not merely paying lip service to the problem but actually addressing it, as many great Christians have already done in the past by living an upright and faithful life *with diligence.*

And as the church unites in our day to confront this great evil, we must remember the unsettling truth that a wide chasm still separates who we desire to be from who we actually are. If we do not constantly try to close that gap, the effects this will have on a sinful, watching world are perilous. We can insult the witness of the church just as much as we can defend it.

Consider, for example, a careless Christian who is hired by a secular company, which believes that because this person follows Jesus, he will be a hard worker. But, rather than working hard on the job, the person uses company time to do church-related tasks such as making copies of bulletins or preparing for Bible studies. How can such a person expect to have a good influence on the holiness of others when he himself leaves diligence behind in the name of his religion and at the expense of his employer? Doing the right things includes doing them *at the right time*. Christians cannot proclaim to live a holy life and then treat those around them with disrespect. For, when they do this, they are no different from hypocrites. The painful reality is, however, that this phenomenon is why many non-Christians do not see the need for Christians to even exist. Does the world really need another group of people whose behavior contradicts their own words?

Put simply, if Christians want to have a positive influence on the world, they cannot live like everyone else; their words cannot war with their actions, for their integrity is the casualty. And non-Christians keep a close eye on our faults. The light of the Christian life is searing to the hearts of creatures lost in sin, so they will take every opportunity they can to drive it away. And what better way to drive back the light than to point out that those who praise its dawning are themselves full of shadow. If those who reject God find even the smallest piece of evidence that we are not who we claim to be, the glory of God will be hidden from them, and the power of true holiness will go elsewhere.

Remember this: the world is not moved and changed merely by Christians who are just as good and live just as diligently as non-Christians. If we are truly children of the heavenly Father, if the wicks of our lives burn with his light, then the lesser lights of the world should seem dark in comparison.

Working for Something Greater Than Money

Notice here that we cannot separate our spiritual lives from our earthly work. We need to be just as diligent in the former as in the latter. What buds in relationship with the triune God should flower in the world of men. And when it does not, we hurt the witness of the church. For example, there was a pastor who proudly shared about a member who loved the church so much that, whenever this person was asked to come to church, the person would drop everything at work and come running. But as I was hearing this, my heart only grew heavy. For the Christian, his or her work is a mission field and calling, not something to be discarded as if it were spiritually irrelevant. It is true that the work of the church far outshines anything that the world strives after, but the purpose of the church is to be a light *in* the world, not a light removed from it. In fact, our greatest testimony to the world can often be our diligence and integrity within it, which is powered by our desire not for more money, but for something far more valuable: consistent Christlikeness.

It is unacceptable to go to work simply to earn money. God wants us to be conforming to Christ's image (Rom 8:29) all the time and in every place, not just when we are in church or at prayer meeting. Surely, time spent at work is what helps us make money, but this time is far more than a means to an end. We work in order to further conform to Christ and thus bring him into every corner of our lives.

There is a story of a politician in England who was always stressed and frustrated by his work. One day, as he pulled up to his house, he saw a street cleaner working in an alley. The cleaner was sweating, and his clothes were modest and sullied, but he was very cheerful and even sang as he was cleaning. Curious about the cleaner's disposition, the politician got out of the car and asked him, "Do you enjoy your work so much that you would sing while you labor?" The cleaner replied, "Yes, I do. For I am cleaning up a corner of the beautiful world that God has created."

I myself worked in the secular world for many years. Before I came to faith, there was a time when I was so fed up with going to work that I considered resigning. But as soon as I met Jesus and was transformed by God's grace, I became thankful for my job, and I looked forward to going to work. In the same way that God was with Joseph in his labor, God was with me. During this time, I shared the gospel as much as I could with my coworkers. We had meals together and developed great camaraderie. And instead of trying to gain an advantage over others, bribing my boss with gifts in order to receive promotions, I worked hard to be someone efficient and useful to the company. I strove to be like Christ in the sense that I would do all I could to be an asset, passionately serving the needs that the company had rather than just doing the bare minimum. I came to work earlier in the morning than others, left work later, and was more focused during the day in carrying out my responsibilities. As I was doing all this, God was with me and with our company. And I was not just working for money. I was working to do all that I could to bring Christ into every corner of my life.

If we want to fix the world, we must seek to become instruments in the hands of the triune God—we need to be effective at addressing the world's problems. That is the only way that our words will have weight, for actions anchor words. If I say that I am *for others* in words alone, the Jesus that I preach will be merely verbal—not the life-altering Jesus of the gospel. Wherever we are, we must seek to be those who are needed, just as Jesus was needed as a carpenter and Paul as a tentmaker.

God has built upon the occupations of his people throughout history for his own purposes—David, we remember, was a shepherd who would eventually learn how to "tend" a nation—so he continues to use our occupations to shape us for his greater kingdom purposes. We will miss out on this shaping work of God if we are foolish enough to live as if sanctification only occurs within the walls of the church. Sanctification happens everywhere and anywhere for Christians.

Do not make the age-old mistake of thinking that serving in the church is more important and precious than living in the world. Dichotomizing the church and the world is something that nonbelievers do, for they cannot see what faith has to do with daily life. But Christians who serve God faithfully in the church know that they must live faithfully outside the church as well, for God is not interested in being Lord of only a part of our lives: he wants all of us. What's more, if we dichotomize the church and the world because we believe that we can segregate sinners and saints, we will be sorely disappointed. Whether in the church or in the world, we are always surrounded by sinners. The world, by God's common grace, is not entirely filthy; just as the church, in God's patience, is not entirely clean.

What we really need to pursue is a life that is *in* the world but not *of* the world, a life that engages with others who reject the God of the Bible while steadily relying on and proclaiming the lordship of that God. If we reverse the former idea—if we are *of* the world and yet pretend not to be *in* it—we do irreparable damage to the church. If we put on the garment of Christ (Rom 13:14) when we tithe, for example, but then cast him aside to manipulate others on our taxes or bribe those above us, we are bringing shame on the name of Christ.

Compounded with our faithful service to Christ in the world is our commitment to him beyond explicitly "Christian" actions. The fact that you open your business with a worship service instead of a traditional shamanistic ritual does not mean that it will be a business that glorifies God. That will depend practically on whether the business functions daily in accordance with the ways of God. We must constantly have a 1 Samuel 15 mentality: to obey is better than sacrifice. Christian rituals do not *establish* Christian character; they *confirm* it. For example, many successful business owners attend Open Door Church, where I serve as pastor. These people properly report all their earnings and pay their taxes. And this is not easy. I do not know how much these people are being taken advantage of by the tax authorities, but although they endure economic and cultural challenges, they desire to be faithful because they believe in the gracious providence of God. And so they come to church as confirmation of their obedient walk with him, not to establish a relationship for which there is no evidence in their professional lives.

Part of the problem here is that we need to know ourselves and be honest about our motives. Making money is not the primary reason we go out into the world and work. Our goal is much more ambitious: to show the world how we as humans are supposed to live. This is the vocation and calling of Christians. This is what we work for, and money pales in comparison.

Eliminating Laziness and Exchanging Dreams for Goals

In light of what we have said about how our work is a witness to the church and how we are working for something far more valuable than money, the peril of laziness should be apparent. Once someone has succumbed to the evil of laziness, the testimony that the world needs to see will never be realized. This is because laziness causes our spiritual and mental health as Christians to deteriorate. That is why, if you have ever interacted with a Christian who struggles with the sin of lethargy, it is difficult to find that person articulating a clear thought.

Perhaps you have heard of Yong Ki Kim, the elder who established Canaan Farmhand School. He has now gone to be with the Lord, but when he was alive, he would rise at four in the morning to pray fervently for the nation and for the people he knew. He clearly instructed and mentored younger men to help them live assiduous and frugal lives. To be this kind of person, one must be diligent and meticulous, not to mention disciplined. One also must be able to clearly and cogently communicate with others. Clear and cogent communication, however, is never the mark of a lazy person. Lethargy turns the mind to mire, and no one wants to wade through mire. That is why the foolish philosophy of people who are lazy never gets very far (except as it spreads to other lazy people!), for they cannot form or articulate healthy and clear thoughts. No one is truly nourished or edified by what they say.

Such a phenomenon is a travesty because it wastes the life we were given. That is precisely where the evil of lethargy lies: in its dismissal of God's gift. And, because of that, while lazy living is damaging to our confidence and harmful to others, it is ultimately a heinous crime against the God who works—who worked to create, and has worked tirelessly ever since then not only to sustain his creation by the word of his power (Heb 1:3), but to redeem us at every second of human history. You cannot claim allegiance to that God and then live a life of lethargy.

But what exactly does a life of lethargy look like? The most noticeable quality in a lazy person is *a lack of advancement and progression* in his or her life. Stagnation is the mark of spiritual languor. This is aptly captured in Proverbs 26:14, which offers a perfect illustration of the lack of progress that marks laziness: "As a door turns on its hinges, so does a sluggard on his bed."

A hinge is the part of a door that controls its opening and closing. When a door is installed, the hinge supports its upright position and allows it to open and close. Without hinges, doors would be more like walls; they would prevent entrance to a desired space.

Now, the text says that the lazy person, like a door that turns on its hinges, turns on his bed. In other words, the bed functions as a hinge for the lazy person. He cannot get out of bed; he can only move where the bed moves. And since beds do not walk, he stays in the same position: no advancement, no movement, no development, no change. Such is the picture of the life of a lazy person.

There is no goal or purpose for someone who has succumbed to a life of lethargy. All his energy is spent, and whatever remains is dedicated to something spiritually worthless, such as material possessions. He may have dreams, but dreams and goals are not the same. A dream is a desire for something. But that is where dreams stop: with desire. A goal, on the other hand, is something that someone burns with passion for and thus strives devotedly to accomplish. For those who have goals, the dream is just the beginning.

Consider an example. Let's say there is a poor man who carries his things around in a knapsack. Because carrying his things is physically taxing and exhausting, he decides to buy a cart in order to make his life easier. Then one day a luxury car whips past him as he saunters down the street, and he says to himself, "Ah, I wish I could ride around in a car like that." In that moment, he has a dream, not a goal. A goal is always accompanied by a detailed plan for achievement. People with goals plan out and organize their lives in such a way that they will eventually achieve their goals. And this is costly. Having lustful thoughts and passing fantasies does not cost us anything but time. Having a goal, however, is expensive, because achieving it requires sacrifice.

Consider a more tangible example. In a recently published

Korean magazine, there was a photo of the feet of a well-known Korean ballerina. Her feet were marked with calluses and scars, so much so that we might not even consider them feet. For her, the cost of the great beauty and grace of ballet was her feet. That was her sacrifice, offered continually through countless hours of practice and performance.

A life-changing goal demands careful and intentional sacrifice. A lazy person is not willing to give something so costly. Therefore, that person stays at home, with his dreams.

A Life with a Simple Goal

What I would like to ask of you is not that you have a complex life with multiple goals, but that you live a simple life with a single, overarching goal: the goal of glorifying God. We must remember here that if one does not live a simple life in this sense, he will likely be unfaithful, because he is torn about what he should accomplish. With a single, overarching goal, we are able to focus, letting go of lesser goals such as self-contentment, comfort, and worldly acceptance.

The great Puritan John Owen believed that the ultimate goal of a genuine Christian was to live a life that had the clear goal of glorifying God. Such a life does not merely talk about God as if he were an idea that others should agree with; rather, a life lived for the glory of God is reorganized and restructured to make daily progress to that end. Fidelity and sincerity meet practicality, and the simple life becomes a life of achievement.

If it were possible to achieve such a life without any effort, it would not be a goal; it would only be a passing action. Someone who wakes up at five thirty to go to a morning prayer meeting has a goal. Someone who decides to sleep until nine and skip morning prayer does not.

Let us return to Proverbs 26:14. Like a door that repeatedly swings on its hinges, a lazy person repeatedly stays in his bed because he has become enslaved to lethargy, and to apathy, its handmaid. A lazy person sees no need for self-control or restructuring, for such things are useless at giving him what he already has.

In the spiritual sense, a person who lives a life without the clear goal of glorifying God chooses to "go with the flow," settling into the current of the world that Christians are made to wade against.

Laziness Disguised as Diligence

At this point, you might be thinking, "Thank God, I am not one of these lazy people. I work diligently every day! I'm always busy!" But this response reveals a critical problem for Christians today. Please do not miss this point: *No matter how busy you may keep yourself each day, if there is no clear goal of living a life for the glory of God, then you are a lazy person.*

There are not many people, after all, who simply roll around in their beds all day. That is not the only kind of lazy person the Bible describes. It also describes as lazy those who fill their schedules completely and thoughtlessly with routines and habits. Think about the Proverbs illustration. A door that is firmly connected to its hinges still turns; in fact, it can be opened and closed quite frequently. But the door never leaves its hinges. It never moves; it simply repeats its motion. There is no change—only repetition.

Likewise, the fact that someone lives a busy life does not mean the person is assiduous in God's eyes. Treading water does not move a person forward or backward. Whenever we do something, we must know *why* we are doing it, and how we can glorify God through it. Otherwise, busyness takes the place of true progress, and we become akin to the door constantly opening and closing on its hinges. Laziness, then, is not measured externally but internally and spiritually.

If we do not know why we are living, then we are not living a God-glorifying life, and this is a matter of the soul. Thoughtless routine does not leave our souls untarnished. It coyly corrodes them so that we become weaker, and then it is easier for us to pretend we are making progress when, in fact, we are not changing at all.

This accounts for the vast number of Christians in our time who *appear* to be busy and seem to accomplish and acquire things. Ironically, it is people without clear and virtuous goals who tend to use busyness as an excuse. In reality, they are, spiritually speaking, doors on hinges. They do not pray; they do not read the Bible; they do not look for opportunities to live out their faith. Does your life resemble this description?

The majority of the people who read this book most likely would not be considered lazy by the world's standards. Many who hold this book in their hands probably rise early every Sunday morning to attend church, and serve wholeheartedly. They may even be people whose nonbelieving friends think they are Jesus freaks who live at church. But, at the end of the day, are they really living a life for God's glory? Is that their goal, or has service become routine?

Even if you never miss a Sunday service, Wednesday worship, or a Friday night prayer meeting, if you are doing these things out of routine and habit, your worship is no different than your job or career. If there is no genuine change in your soul, no honest suffering, no earnest concern, no desire to know the truth, then your life is not being shaped by the grace of God.

And if you are living this way—even if all your friends and family consider you diligent and devoted and respect you for this—in God's eyes, you are still a door turning on its hinges.

Red Bean Bread

People whose lives resemble a turning door—who carry on a steady and repetitive lifestyle without true progress—are not really living their lives. They are being led around by something else, trapped in habitual wandering. You can spend yourself living this way under the illusion that you are truly busy, but because none of it has been for the Lord, it is tantamount to a life of lethargy.

And if we continue to live without clear and intentional goals, and work hard simply because we think there are no other options, our lives are like red bean bread without the red bean filling: the shell is appealing, but there is nothing sustaining and valuable on the inside.[1] So, no matter how much you travel without resting

---

1 Red bean bread is a popular treat in Korea. A suitable American analogue would
  be a jelly doughnut.–Trans.

or work without taking a break, you are not progressing in your walk with God and you are not busy with things that matter. Your relationship with him is deteriorating, and your heart will only grow more troubled with time. But we can be tempted, in our disillusionment, to try to solve the problem by working even more in our routine. But that just means the door will swing more frequently on its hinges; our hearts will be void and troubled and never satisfied because we are chasing temporal dreams rather than heavenly goals.

And, as we said earlier, a life without goals is an empty life—a life of shallow dreams—and this will only lead to spiritual fatigue. Such fatigue marks a life governed by someone other than God, who always gives us the energy and resources to do the work to which he has called us. Apart from him, all work leads to a tired soul and a body exhausted by banalities. What's worse, when we find ourselves in this condition, even essential tasks appear to be duties, rather than things in which we find joy, and so our standards are lowered. We desire to do only the bare minimum. We become shells of our true selves; we turn into swinging doors.

Even when we try to be convicted by a message or sermon and learn something from Scripture, there is still no progress in our lives. Instead, we treat the life-changing spiritual truths of Scripture as if they were ideas God is calling us to agree with. All this comes about because we do not want to step outside our comfort zones and be challenged. In such frustration, it becomes impossible to develop sacrificial and devoted faith. Lethargy becomes a breeding ground for lust and personal desires that end in nothing.

And once we are caught by this chimera—once we fall prey to

living a goal-less, regular, and ordinary life—it is only a matter of time before our souls wither. More perilous is the fact that even the prayers of such a person cannot have the heart-wrenching genuineness that God demands. Indeed, how could prayers of a lazy person have this? In order to have passionate prayer requests, we must have unfulfilled goals that we long to achieve, but such people have no goals. They only have dreams, and so no amount of begging from Christian brothers and sisters can get them to pursue godly goals. Consider the weight, then, of this problem for the church today! For if we resign ourselves to living regular lives, the gospel content that we profess is sapped of its vigor and only the formal church remains, a distant and embarrassing reflection of the historical beacon it once was. Authenticity wanes, tradition waxes, and the church is left spiritually destitute and dim in a world that will shrivel and die without a light to follow. This must not be allowed to happen.

Finding a Goal, Faithfulness, and Diligence

If we want to avoid this, if we want to avoid being seen as lazy in God's eyes, we must first have clear and specific goals. Second, we must live faithfully and ardently to achieve those goals. It is really that simple, even though the process seems complex in practice.

We can learn a lot about others and ourselves from mere observation. Focusing on others for a moment, we can learn many things from observing how hard someone works. And if the one observing someone happens to be that person's manager or superior, he or she can shape the person's habits and work ethic to optimize productivity and efficiency. But some people cannot be shaped this way. They continually need their work checked and even finished for them owing to negligence or ignorance. This type of person is not faithful, for he or she only works to please him- or herself. And if the self is always the object of gratification, others are bound to suffer.

One of the ways in which others suffer from the work of a lazy person is as a result of that person's inconsistency. If someone says that he will attend morning prayer daily and does so without exception—regardless of who is watching—he is the epitome of faithfulness. He does what he does for God's glory and in God's sight. Certainly, we cannot always be perfectly consistent, for we are still sinners, on top of the fact that life is unpredictable and missing a morning prayer service may be inevitable. But a truly faithful person makes that the rare exception, not the norm.

This means that living a diligent life involves not just consistency but also persistence—that is, perseverance. Perseverance does not mean that we stop when we no longer want to continue; it means we stop when we are *no longer able* to continue. Perseverance means pushing through adversity and hardship in order to reach one's goal, relying on the Spirit to drive oneself through the difficult times. This perseverance is central to the diligence we need to cultivate in order to achieve our goals. It is, in this sense, a Christlike cultivation of diligence because, on a far smaller scale, it means we follow Christ's path of suffering unto glory—pushing through humiliation and adversity, even ridicule, in order to achieve the goal.

Along with such Christlike perseverance is what we have been calling, more strictly, diligence: continual and sustained passion and focus in order to attain a goal.

From work to public service to maintaining one's relationship with the Lord, a Christian must be prepared to be faithful and diligent—making sacrifices for the glory of God and thus being shaped more and more into Christ's image.

Laziness as the Soul's Bane

The heart of a person with Christlike diligence reflects the light of God to others. When he encounters the people around him, they begin to wonder whether they are missing something from their own lives.

But what light can people offer the world, which daily faces the horrendous adversity of life without the light of Christ, if they drop everything and quit at the slightest hint of adversity? This is just as bad as being spiritually numb, for it is through anguish and adversity that we are shaped into Christ and forced, against the wishes of our old sinful heart, to depend on God. Adversity is the catalyst for Christlike change.

Before that change comes, one recognizes how useless he is, and is humbled in every way. Only when his own strength is shattered can he have true strength in Christ (2 Cor 12:10). Sometimes we find ourselves asking, "How could someone as flawed and deficient as I am live my life not in vain, but truly for the glory of God?" When such questions arise, we are one step closer to being an instrument in the hands of the God who is always working. We may still feel like a door turning on its hinges at the beginning of this process, but God has already begun to work on us by his Spirit, renewing us in the image of his Son as those who work for his glory.

The danger for someone who keeps busy on the outside but who, on the inside, is lazy in God's eyes is that his soul will become tired. To the world, this does not matter because it is not easy for the world to recognize. In the world's eyes, there is not much difference between a person whose soul is enduring much anguish but diligently accepting challenges and a person who merely works hard at maintaining a routine. The world does not see as God sees; worldly people are blind to spiritual realities.

And, to make matters more difficult, the fact that one has received grace does not guarantee that one's life will dramatically improve on the outside. Commitments and routines remain in place. If you are working, you still need to work. If you are a stay-at-home mom, you still need to pour your life into your children. As long as you did not arouse criticism or stir up controversy or burn bridges with your neighbors, you will still need to interact with them. The daily routine you had before Christ changed your life does not disappear. Your perspective on it may change, but it does not disappear.

In light of how external realities remain even when someone undergoes a dramatic internal change, it makes sense that other people cannot always distinguish between nominal Christians who are lazy in God's eyes but busy in the world's eyes and genuine Christians who are truly busy suffering hardship and adversity for the glory of God. This is why it is so easy to simply act as a spectator of the problem of laziness: no one will criticize us for seeming to be busy. In fact, people will often praise us. And that is how laziness can go unnoticed and eventually become the bane of our souls.

In God's eyes, however, there are really only two types of people: those who are dead and those who are living. The difference between the two cannot be wholly put into words, but we can at least say that those who are alive are truly *in* his Son, while those who are dead are still in Adam (Rom 5:12–18). The latter brings insult and grief to God, while the former brings much glory to him.

Reorienting Your Life to the Soul's Needs

The simple fact is that we cannot be lazy as Christians—physically or spiritually. We must prioritize what is most important in our lives (bringing glory to God), and then organize everything else accordingly.

We cannot wait until our environment or circumstances get better. The enemy will always use our circumstances against us, and we must seek to overcome them. It is never circumstances that wreck or ruin our lives, but laziness in our soul and flesh is oftentimes the culprit.

Spiritual laziness destroys our souls by anesthetizing us in our relationship with the God who is always working. And, as others see our lives as poor models, their faith will be threatened as well. The influence of one person's laziness is never neatly contained. It spills over into the lives of others.

To readers of this book, I want to ask you, "Are you living a purposeless, repetitive, and exhausting life in any sense?" Even if you feel very busy, is there any chance that God's glory is not the goal you are pursuing? Are you trying to serve God faithfully and yet you lack a personal relationship with him? If any of these questions strike close to home, then please remember that no matter how faithful and dedicated you think you are, you are not really a diligent person. I say this not to insult you, but to keep you from greater dangers. The life you live may be a perfect picture of Proverbs 26:14—a door turning on its hinges.

Do not look at your life as the world does; examine your soul deeply and try to diagnose yourself carefully and candidly. Listen attentively to what your soul is wrestling with, and lay your true desires on the table. Do you truly want to glorify God with your life?

2

Robbed by a Thief

(Proverbs 22:13)

In the previous chapter, we found that labor has been part and par
cel of our creaturely existence since the beginning, even before the
fall. All our negative associations about work have come from the
effects of sin. Sin, in its manifold manifestations, has given us
the false impression that work is something to be avoided, and the
world has reinforced this impression. Self-centered ambition is
the world's disguise for what is, in fact, laziness in God's eyes, for
all work that is not done for God's glory is idle work. This truth was
drawn from our consideration of Proverbs 26:14, "As a door turns
on its hinges, so does a sluggard on his bed." A door can turn frequently on its own hinges without going anywhere, just as a person
can do worldly work without making any spiritual progress. Within
this fallen world, a world in which spiritual laziness is overlooked as
material ambition, the Christian church is called to be a light in the
darkness. It is the duty of the church to show that work is indeed

something to value because of its God-given roots. True and lasting work—work that is done for the glory of God, and carried out with persevering diligence—is something that reflects the ever-working triune God of Scripture. If we are to bring glory to this God, we must begin exchanging worldly dreams for heavenly goals. In short, we must begin to cultivate Christ-centered diligence.

In this chapter, we continue our exploration of what Christ-centered diligence entails, and we begin by looking at another passage from Proverbs that brings to our attention the quiet evil of laziness. But before we get to that, we start with a story.

Robbed by a Thief

A long time ago, there lived a very lazy farmer. One day, while everyone else went out to the fields to work, he decided to loiter around in his house and do absolutely nothing. Hours passed, and eventually he decided to lie down on the bamboo floor and take an afternoon nap. While he was sleeping, he heard strange, furtive noises. Curious about what was making the noise, he lazily opened his eyes. "Perhaps," he thought, "there is a thief foolish and daring enough to try to rob me in broad daylight." He drifted back to sleep. But the sound he had heard was, indeed, a thief who had kicked a rock loose while he climbed down the inside of the farmer's wall. Shortly after entering the property, the thief was in plain view of the farmer, who saw him scampering around his fields. But instead of being startled and getting up, he muttered, "It's just a thief . . . God help him if he comes near my garden." And, once more, he drifted back to sleep.

Moments later there was a loud bang. The farmer groggily opened his eyes and saw the thief creeping toward the garden. But he gave in to his heavy eyelids. "He'd better not come inside," he grumbled, and then fell back to sleep. The thief saw that the farmer was sleeping heavily, and very quietly came into the house. He passed by the farmer on the floor and went into the main room. Once more, the farmer awoke. But instead of getting up to challenge the thief, he mumbled, "That fool is in the main room—he'd better not take anything."

Shortly thereafter, the thief gathered everything valuable he could find— silverware, jewelry, expensive food, spices—and filled a large knapsack. Then he made his way out of the farmer's house, without giving him a second thought. He passed the garden and walked right through the main gate. Awakening once more, the farmer lifted up his head to see the thief strolling away, but he refused to trouble himself by getting up. Instead, he shut his eyes and said to himself, "I dare him to come back . . ."

The Sluggard's Tongue Is Busy

In Proverbs 22:13, a sluggard is described as someone who does not want to leave his house for fear that a lion will kill him in the streets. In today's world, most jobs are done inside temperature-controlled buildings, behind desks and in front of computer screens, so we might have trouble imagining the original context. When this Scripture was written, Israel was an agrarian society, where everyone had to work outdoors. Even if one could carry on his trade inside a building, he would have to go outside in order to sell his products. Therefore, anyone who refused to go out was likely either sick or committed to loafing around places of comfort.

The Hebrew word used in the text is *atsēl*, which is derived from the verb *atsal*. Although it is translated as "lazy," *atsal* can be taken as idling around, delaying or postponing, and hesitating. One of the intentions of the author of Proverbs was that the book be a collection of lessons to be mastered in the context of everyday life. If this is the case, then what would his goal be for the proverbs he wrote criticizing lazy people? As we might imagine, his desire was that the sluggard start being concerned about his daily life as well as his spiritual well-being. That is why, in the passage, the author of Proverbs is pointing out that the sluggard is merely thinking of ways to avoid his duties and making excuses.

But do not assume that the sluggard's *tongue* is lazy just because he is a sluggard. The lazier the sluggard, the more he moves his tongue. That is one of sin's ironies: when the rest of the body lies limp, the tongue travails—laboring to excuse, to criticize, to insult. Consider the story I just told. The only action that the farmer took was with his tongue. Aside from his words, the farmer was nearly lifeless. Perhaps you were not surprised as you read the story: it seems that many lazy people can reel off rhetoric, but they never say anything worth remembering. So it is with the sluggard in Proverbs 22:13. He *says*, "There is a lion outside! I shall be killed in the streets!" He is so determined not to work that he gives an outrageous excuse for not leaving his house.

What is it that causes people to make so many excuses, especially when they know that laziness is a bad thing? And they *do* know it is a bad thing. Think about it: the negative connotations of laziness transcend age, gender, ethnicity, and religion. Everyone everywhere knows that idleness and lethargy are undesirable. Laziness receives universal condemnation. So why would people disregard its evil and bask in it? The answer is simple, but potentially offensive: because there is an intrinsic deficiency in them— they have fallen deeply in love with themselves. They would never admit this, nor would they use these words to diagnose their condition. But it is true, and as long as it is true, they will continue to tangle themselves in the web of sloth. The only way to tear themselves away from this web is if they diligently and consistently labor for God's glory.

The Balance between Work and Rest

But let me be clear: I do not mean to say that everyone should always be busy. Even godly people who are faithful to God need seasons of rest, and this is mandated by God himself (see Gen 2:2). Because working involves the body and soul, it is a godly thing to give your mind and body rest when you are exhausted. God did not create us to bear up under stress forever. Even before the fall, we would have rested from our work, for God rests after his good work of creation, and we are made in his image (Gen 1:26). Once sin entered God's good world, it accentuated our finitude and frailty, making rest absolutely critical. If we needed rest before the fall, how much more so do we need it when we are plagued by fatigue, stress, injuries, and a host of other issues! In this sense, we need to make sure we are allowing ourselves to rest—both in mind and in body.

But there is a fine line between rest and laziness. It is wise to take a day off to get some well-deserved rest if one feels exhausted from overworking. But using rest as a pretext to miss a Bible study, prayer meeting, or Sunday worship is another matter, especially because these events are ultimately aimed at giving us rest, for true and eternal rest is found in the triune God alone. As Augustine confessed hundreds of years ago, "Our heart is unquiet until it rests in you."[1] We cannot dodge regular meetings with other members of the body of Christ under the pretext that we need rest, for we then would be sacrificing eternal rest in order to find temporal rest! When we find ourselves thinking this way, we must recognize it for what it is: sluggishness—the very same attitude of the sluggard who refuses to go out for fear of being torn apart by a lion. We might be tempted to give excuses not to serve in the church or partake of its ministry because we fear that the lion of fatigue will overtake us. But what we think is a lion will turn out to be a house cat once our communion in the body of Christ brings us before the Lion of the tribe of Judah (Rev 5:5).

This brings up an important point—something we must know in order to more effectively resist the temptation to rest when we should be engaged in spiritually invigorating work. We need to approach decisions about rest and work with a clear understanding of our fallen nature and the sinful habits we have developed as a result. It is precisely because of our indwelling sin that we seek our own advancement and agendas. We constantly gravitate toward the idol of self-fulfillment because we have a sad and stubborn

---

1 Augustine, *The Works of Saint Augustine I/1, Confessions,* trans. Maria Boulding (New York: New City Press, 2004), 39.

history of serving ourselves rather than God and his kingdom. We might start by asking the question, "Am I resting because I *need* to rest in order to better serve God and others, or am I resting because *I don't want* to serve?" Consistently asking and candidly answering this question can help us discern when rest is necessary and when perseverance is called for. But this ability to discern can only be obtained if we begin with a proper understanding of ourselves as fallen creatures—creatures who are prone to serving themselves.

Again, let me emphasize that rest is a necessity. Because we are not immortal, we must know our limits: how much can we work, and how much stress and strain can we endure physically and spiritually? The answers to these questions will differ from person to person, depending on the nature of our work, additional life circumstances, and so on. But each of us must ask these questions and answer them honestly on a regular basis. That way, we can practice discerning whether the desires we have for rest are coming from our finite, creaturely nature or from of our sinful, self-serving nature.

We need to practice this discernment for ourselves so that we become skilled in assessing when we long for good, creaturely rest and when we long for sinful, selfish rest (laziness). Let me give you an example of why such practice is necessary. In our neighborhood, we frequently encounter very physically weak people. It is very sobering to see them struggle, and we empathize with their weakness because we, too, know what it is like to be weak or broken. But some of these people suffer internally because they cannot tell the difference between good rest and selfish rest (laziness). For instance, an elderly woman may have a walking routine each day, but then one day she develops a sharp pain in her lower back. Now she must choose: will she stop and rest or keep walking? If she chooses to sit down on a bench, is she doing so because she is *unable* to walk (or might worsen her injury if she does walk) or because she is *unwilling* to walk? Tormented by not wanting to appear lazy, she may continue walking and worsen her injury. Or she may rest on the bench but feel guilty and defeated as she does so, thinking that she has given in to laziness. Now she is trapped between a fear of laziness and a fear of work. She has paralyzed her conscience. Ultimately, only this woman herself can know whether she is pursuing good rest or laziness.

In this sense, all throughout our lives, we must learn to restrain ourselves and check our assumptions, prayerfully relying on the Spirit to help us resist the lure of our sinful nature. If we do not do this—if we live carelessly and thoughtlessly, never examining our souls to see what deception and misunderstanding reside there— make no mistake: we will be daily deceived by sin. The devil will claim battles in the war that our Savior has already won; we will be taken advantage of, and we will fail to work as unto the Lord (Col 3:23).

The Root of Laziness: Love for Oneself

But now let us return to what we said earlier, since it has a bearing on our ability to discern when we should work and when we should rest: *the ultimate cause of laziness is love of oneself.* While we have seen that we can easily be deceived by sin with regard to discerning the proper times for work and rest, this deception is not the root of our desire to be lazy. The root of our desire to be lazy is self-love. This is important to note, since a person who is considered lazy is not incapable of doing hard work. No matter how lazy someone is, he will always work diligently if it is work he truly wants to do. Rather, what that person must ask himself, and what we must ask ourselves daily, are two questions: (1) Is the work we are doing work that we love? (2) Is it work for God and his kingdom rather than work that only serves ourselves?

Consider someone who spends his days only watching television. One day, as he is sunk in his lounge chair watching his favorite show, the television screen suddenly goes black and the audio cuts out. He pauses briefly and then jumps to his feet in order to investigate the problem. If it is his connection, he will call his cable company and stay on the line until he is assured that he will have his TV up and running again. If the problem is with the television itself, he will gladly carry it to his car and drive it to a repair shop. What caused this sudden urgency to act? Why was laziness so quickly exchanged for labor? Was it because he had a passion to fix the connection or mechanical problem? No, not really. Even though he jumped up and did everything in his power to resolve the situation, he is still lazy because of his *motivation*. His answer to the second question we posed above is, "It serves only myself." He was busy for selfish reasons. And that means that, in an ultimate sense, he is still lazy; he is still ignoring the work in his soul that needs to be done: the work of God. It is in this sense that the ultimate root of laziness is love for oneself.

And remember this: if a person's life revolves around himself, he will remain lazy no matter how hard he may work. We are all ultimately lazy if we cannot answer *both* of the above questions to God's satisfaction. A positive answer to only the first question means that we are busy for self; a negative answer to the second question means we are lazy for God. And that is precisely why no one who is considered lazy has a vigorous spiritual life. All the great spiritual men and women that we read about in Scripture were diligent, self-sacrificing servants of God. That is why he used them to accomplish great things for his name's sake. There was no reason for God to give such beautiful and redemptively critical tasks to sluggards. Such tasks would be wasted on people who love themselves more than they love God.

While it may sound abrasive, there is a reason why I am saying that the root of laziness is love for oneself: self-centeredness is an evil that corrodes the lives of others. It cannot be neatly contained in one's own life. A similar phenomenon occurs with laziness: it breaks down relationships. The self-love of laziness is not only harmful to the person who is lazy, it is harmful to those he loves— or to those who love him. Laziness lacerates our relationships; it cuts them with carelessness. Just consider a lazy person in your own family. Don't the effects of that person's behavior (or lack of behavior!) reach everyone else? If a husband and father is lazy, his entire family will suffer. If a wife and mother is lazy, her husband and children will suffer. If a child is lazy, his or her parents will suffer. Laziness is never neatly confined to an individual. It wreaks havoc on relationships.

Scripture confirms as much. It describes the trustworthy and faithful person as a refreshing drink in the time of harvest, while the sluggard is like smoke to the eyes and vinegar to the teeth (Prov

25:13, 10:26). In other words, a faithful person is refreshing to others, while the sluggard becomes their burden.

Understanding Self-Love

Self-love constantly puts obstacles in the way of godly and holy living. This is because the one who loves himself places his own interests, agenda, and desires above those of God. In other words, the laziness of humanity ultimately causes people to stop thinking of God's glory as a worthwhile pursuit, and encourages them to cherish instead a more comfortable life. In effect, it reverses the opening statement of the Westminster Shorter Catechism: rather than our chief end being "to glorify God, and to enjoy him forever," we practically live as if our chief end is "to glorify self, and to ignore God indefinitely."

But this is an old, old story for us. To live ultimately for ourselves seems instinctual—no one has to teach a child how to be selfish; all you have to do is grip the toy he has in his hands and watch his smile turn to a frown. Almost without exception, he will blurt out the word that encapsulates human sin: "Mine!" We might balk at a toddler's selfishness, but we are often no better as adults. We are bent on looking out for ourselves and our possessions before we look to the needs of others, and it has been this way ever since the fall of mankind. And yet, at the same time, it is also clear that there are people who are very hard on themselves—to the point of abuse. This phenomenon can be attributed to a misunderstanding of how one is supposed to properly love oneself. We know, of course, that all people love themselves (Matt 22:39), but no person has the power to love himself completely without God. This is because to love oneself completely requires the ability to be aware of and understand (1) where one is in life and what one's goals are *for God*, (2) the nature of the love one receives from God, and (3) the happiness that results from receiving that love. All these components make one aware of and foster a desire for fulfilling one's duty to bring glory to God as part of his creation. Without this proper orientation, no one can love himself completely without falling into selfish ambitions. Ignoring God in the pursuit of self-love only leads to a distortion of what love truly is.

Consider, for example, the countless people who live promiscuous and decadent lives. This lifestyle can be attributed not merely to the effects of sin, but more specifically to a distortion of what love really is. Bound up with our ability to love ourselves truly is the ability to understand and be aware of our life's position and goal (which ultimately must be oriented toward God's plan for redemption), the nature of the love we receive from God, and the unending joy we have in receiving that love. Glorifying God for this great and eternal love is what marks us as his creatures. And even here, in our attempts to live out true love, the notion of work is present, for all of this—finding our life's goal, understanding and finding joy in the love God has for us—requires Spirit-wrought initiative on our part. And it is precisely a lack of this initiative that leads to selfish ambition, and that selfish ambition when acted upon, leads people to live promiscuous and decadent lives: promiscuous, because they have lost sight of the only one who can give them purpose and love (God himself); decadent, because losing sight of the living God only leads to corruption and moral decay. A promiscuous and decadent lifestyle is not merely the result of poor decisions; it is the natural outworking of the rejection of true love—biblical love—along with the direction and sacrifice such love requires.

However—and this is critical if we are to maintain a biblical faith—healing and redemption for such people (and we should daily remind ourselves that before the Spirit led us to Christ, we were all in the category of "such people") is not simply a matter of working harder to accept God's love. We can only embrace God's love, and thus more fully love ourselves as his creatures, if we are reborn by the Spirit. We need, in other words, Trinitarian trans-formation: the will of the Father and the work of the Son must be infused in us by a second birth of the Spirit. That is the only way we can be shaped in our desires, our thoughts, and our emotions—all oriented toward loving service of God, others, and ourselves. It is only with this Spirit-wrought renewal that we come to know the purpose of our existence. And it is here that we realize the profound truth that self-love—love that is biblically prescribed and purposely enjoyed—is actually an instrument that brings glory to God.

When someone properly experiences God's love in this way and becomes intimate with his character, that person will not be so immersed in himself. Self-love, paradoxically, turns to a focus on God and others. Once creatures who are reborn in Christ witness how God loved them, their life's goals will be reoriented, turning away from themselves and toward the God who gave himself for his creatures. Ultimately, this is because reborn creatures decide to live for God, and any self-love such creatures have is ultimately concerned not with self-satisfaction but with God-satisfaction—that is, with bringing glory to God.

And here is where the pain and peril of humanity lie: for those who never know the real reason for their existence, for those who have never experienced God's love, their love remains misdirected. It remains, more accurately, a *selfish* love. This is why love that is not rooted in God leads only to a vain search for the satisfaction of one's own pleasure. In such lives, grace loses ground, and sin continues to grow. It is this very truth that the author of Proverbs wanted to warn the sluggard about. Hiding from the responsibility and initiative that biblical self-love requires leads to spiritual stagnation, and ultimately to selfish love.

God's Labor through Human Labor

But lest we feel intimidated by such responsibility, Christians find comfort in the truth that our God is Immanuel: the "with us" God. God himself takes responsibility for the lives of his people; he always gives us exactly what we need in order to live a loving life for his glory. And we should not be so surprised by this. He who cares so passionately for creation would never abandon his image-bearing creatures to their own ends. What kind of king would feed the birds of the air and clothe the lilies of the field, but neither feed nor clothe his own people? This is what Scripture says: "But if God so clothes the grass, which is alive in the field today, and tomorrow is thrown into the oven, how much more will he clothe you, O you of little faith! And do not seek what you are to eat and what you are to drink, nor be worried" (Luke 12:28–29).

Take note in this passage of an obvious but often-ignored truth: God works through the hard work and labor of humans.

The passage is not teaching that we are to be idle like a person who waits at the bottom of an apple tree for fruit to fall down. To do the equivalent of this in our spiritual lives would be to abuse the grace of God. It would be, in some sense, connected to the sin of Adam and Eve, who abused God's gracious provision in the garden. We cannot simply request that God hand us a fruitful life. That sort of laziness, though often pawned off as prayerful piety, destroys not only the flesh, but the soul as well. God grants us such a life *only as we labor with him.*

And as we labor with him, we will find that the toil of labor is a treasured part of our spiritual growth, for labor constantly shows us how much God is doing in our lives and the lives around us. Consider the staggering optimism of Christians who have had to work tirelessly throughout their lives, and contrast them with pessimistic lazy people. You will quickly find that optimism is a character trait to which laborers are privy. Not so with those stuck in a lazy lifestyle. Anyone who is caught in a web of laziness and yet who is also optimistic likely has this attitude not because of careful reflection, but because of a refusal to really think about his or her life's purpose. Laziness makes us *worse* than instinct-driven animals. An animal has an instinct to survive and spends its time trying to do so. A lazy human being, on the other hand, has a God-given instinct to thrive and yet ignores it for cheaper pleasures. In seeking after those cheap pleasures, he finds himself less optimistic about what life has to offer and more pessimistic about what he can attain. Laziness bleeds the well of optimism dry. So, you see, the issue of laziness is not simply an issue of taking up a role in society to earn money. It runs far deeper than that; it percolates through the soil of the spirit. Our willingness to labor and toil reflects a heartfelt attempt to labor with God in doing the good work he has planned for us. Our refusal to labor and toil is an evil.

Remember what we noted earlier: labor is not a punishment of the fall, but something that God had ordained for humans to do even before sin entered the world. God's glory will be revealed through the labor of humanity. Conversely, Satan's rebellion will be manifested through our refusal to lift a finger. But this truth seems so counterintuitive to creatures living in a fallen world— where work is so often looked at as a mere means to a monetary end. That is why some people think that if Adam and Eve hadn't eaten from the tree of the knowledge of good and evil, we would all be in the garden of Eden resting and relaxing. But a brief glance at Genesis 2:19–20 makes it unequivocally clear that Adam and Eve were laboring in the Garden *before* sin entered into it. Adam labored greatly: he named every single beast of the field and bird of the air, and was given charge of the entire earth—the grandest administrative task ever given in human history! If sin had not entered into the world, we would be in the garden of Eden working joyfully during the day and getting some good rest at night. Labor itself is not a punishment; it is a divine gift granted by the God who labors out of love. But toiling and bitter fruit are God's judgment because of sin. We have been living in the latter context for so long that we have forgotten our origin. We must begin to revisit that Genesis context repeatedly in order to remind ourselves of the goodness—the joy—of laboring for God's glory.

And when we think about the work done in the garden of Eden, there is a relevant lesson that we can glean with regard to our labor in the twenty-first century. If the flourishing of the garden of Eden required labor even without sin, then one can only imagine how much more work would be required to restore God's creation after the fall. This is why we cannot be lazy. We must instead be diligent and faithful in all areas of our life, for the creation that longed for our labor before sin is now groaning for it in the midst of redemption (see Rom 8:22).

Whenever I travel to the US or Europe, I notice many things that I believe should be emulated by the Korean culture and government. The biggest out of all of these is a social welfare system. In the US and Europe, social welfare systems were not established to financially save people forever. They weren't even established to provide financial relief for those who are mentally handicapped or live with autism. These governments went out of their way and invested resources into establishing relatively simple labor systems to encourage these citizens to work. If these countries didn't have this kind of system, then all these citizens would have to receive government aid until death. And it was not because the governments didn't have the funds to support this group of people that they decided to form welfare programs. Rather, these governments were willing to invest great resources in such programs in order to provide temporary assistance and empower people to find gainful employment.

It seems that the US and Europe understand the intrinsic value of labor. This is why they give the somewhat easier manual labor jobs to those who are mentally handicapped or specially abled. Even if expected results are not achieved, just as they are not achieved in many areas of labor, people are given plenty of time to be trained properly, and paid fairly for their work. This opportunity was made available so that all people would have a chance to work and earn money to pay bills, put a roof over their heads, and put food on the table. This also empowers these workers to believe that they are important members of society and are making a significant contribution to it—and they are, in a striking and biblical way! They are living out their image-bearing responsibility to labor for God's glory. And note that following through on this responsibility makes people personally realize their worth as human beings, crafted and shaped by the God of loving labor. This is because it is through labor that they will have a clear understanding of their purpose for existing: bringing glory to the God who is always working. It is when we expend our energy and efforts that we find joy in our purpose. Echoing the psalmist, "You shall eat the fruit of the labor of your hands" (Ps 128:2), we are compelled to say that labor is a means of grace that God has blessed us with. We eat the fruit of the labor of our hands just as God, in a far more mysterious and wonderful way, enjoys the fruit of his own labor in creation, especially the communion his creatures have with him in Christ, by the power of the Spirit. God *loves* the fruit of his redemptive labor in Christ—that is, us!

The Call to an Exhausting Life as a Spiritual Blessing

Are you beginning to see how this changes our outlook on all our work? And it's not just our physical labor we have in mind, but our spiritual labor as well. The blessing of labor is not limited to the physical life. As a matter of fact, it extends in profound ways to our spiritual life.

The reason why labor is such a spiritual blessing is that it contributes to one's pursuit of holiness. As I mentioned earlier, once, when my struggles with sin were difficult to bear, I thought to myself, "Why did God make the process of sanctification so difficult and hard to endure? He could have just completed the process the moment he saved me. He could have made me like an angel—spotless and perfect. That way, I wouldn't have to stay in this world as long." But as time passed, I came to realize that the daunting and arduous process of sanctification is truly a blessing. This is because in the midst of his sins and struggles, the believer has every idol stripped from him, along with every false assumption about what is truly valuable. In the pangs of sanctification, we are brought to realize with utter clarity that pursuing God is our only end—what the Westminster Confession of Faith calls our "chief and highest end." This is what God had originally intended for humanity to keep in their hearts, and as long as they did so they were faithful and obedient. This is the state that God desires us to return to, and if God had not ordained for us to endure such an arduous process of sanctification, humanity would have decayed far more quickly. But because God has given us the mission to endure this difficult process of conforming more and more to Christ's image, we do not need to become discouraged or arrogant during our time on earth. We have not obtained the prize, nor are we perfect, but we are able to live diligently day by day because of the foundation of grace (Phil 3:12).

But do we really possess this godly assiduity? Perhaps better: Do we even ask the Spirit for it? Simply having many tasks to do does not mean we are ardent workers. Everyone has different duties and jobs to fulfill, but there is no point in someone just doing what he or she must do with little care, effort, or concern. We need to fulfill our duties and responsibilities with dedication and discipline, in prayerful reliance on the Spirit of the living, laboring God.

This is very difficult for us, not simply because we often forget to ask the Spirit for God's help in working diligently, but because we are overloaded with tasks. There are very few people who only have one responsibility or job to do; most people have many roles they must play: a young man, for example, is simultaneously a worker at a corporation, the head of a household, the volunteer coach of a soccer team, and a leader in the local church. In the midst of so many responsibilities, therefore, most people first need to take on duties and responsibilities that do not waste time. In other words, we need to refrain from doing what someone else could do more devotedly and with more vigor and attention than we could possibly offer. If we stubbornly hold on to every task that comes our way, we will not be able to properly handle all our duties and responsibilities. And, in the end, we will be confronted with the reality that we are just going from one task to another without any real purpose or significance. It is easy in such circumstances to become oblivious to the blessings or company that God is offering us. What's more, we leave behind the experience of being spiritually inundated with the cool, refreshing waters of God's grace in our work. We are not revitalized by our labor, but only torn down by it. And, to our detriment and God's grief, we become like vinegar to God's teeth and smoke to his eyes (Prov 10:26).

"There are so many things I have to do, but I only have one

body. I have no time. That's why I can't do as much." How many times have we uttered words like these? We have no justification for making these excuses in front of God. No one has two bodies, or more or less time than 24 hours in a day. We're all creatures living in God's world. What we must do rather than complain about our responsibilities is *prioritize* them, and admit that the issue is not a lack of time, but a lack of spiritual foresight (preparation and time management), diligence, and discipline.

The Call to Diligence and the Body of Christ

But, we seem pressed to ask, how does one cultivate diligence? It is clear that it cannot be simply taught. Instead, it must be developed and accompanied by Spirit-driven wisdom. What this means is having the sense and awareness to know and harmoniously balance what is important and necessary work and what is not. The solution is not simply becoming better at organizing our schedule. That would undoubtedly help many people, but it does not address the heart of the matter. The solution is prayerfully planning and managing our responsibilities so that we do what is necessary with the time we have.

We can always be better at this; everyone should strive to become more diligent than they are—from the major tasks we take on to the ordinary chores we do: we could all clean and do dishes more quickly and efficiently. When we finish the tasks we need to accomplish more quickly, we are earning more time. If someone does the same task or duty for many years without having developed more efficient techniques or procedures to complete it, that proves that the work was done without the necessary thought, care, or concern. It is instinctual for people to try to do worthwhile tasks more efficiently and quickly by developing different techniques or procedures; this, among many other things, is what separates humans from animals.

Laziness calls us into a coma; it keeps us from creatively and persistently analyzing what we do and how we do it. In fact, it encourages us to find excuses *not* to do what we are called to do. Diligence calls us to rethink, reimagine, reinvent—to search for ways to innovate for the sake of efficiency without compromising effectiveness. This call to diligence—a call voiced by the Spirit of God himself—can enable us to develop diligence into a habit. And that habit is what makes up for time lost in laziness.

However, we need others in the body of Christ to help us become more efficient. I recall an instance when I tried to change the size of footnotes in a document I was working on. I was inefficient at this task, changing one footnote at a time. The student who came in and showed me how to change the size of all my footnotes in a matter of seconds was helping me become remarkably more efficient. Because of this insight, I saved time—precious time. It was then that I realized humility always has a home with diligence. If we refuse to humble ourselves and let others teach us, our personal attempts at diligence will only be so effective. Labor happens best in community—just as it did with Adam and Eve in the garden.

And paired with our reliance on others is our need to continually assess ourselves and the roles in which God has placed us. I have different roles I am called upon to play—as a preacher, shepherd, researcher, writer, and so on. You likely have many roles to play yourself. Sometimes people ask me how I am able to work at everything God has called me to, and the answer I have is simple: I have learned to distinguish between essential and nonessential tasks. I do what I *must* do, not what I *think I could* do. There are certain things that I have learned I must delegate to others who can do them more efficiently and effectively than I could. And when I find myself facing a task that I *must* do—an essential task—I strive to find ways to complete it as quickly and effectively as possible. I even make this part of my prayer life: I ask God to help me discern between essential and nonessential tasks, and to complete the essential tasks for his glory, without wasting time.

What's more, I have found that this approach to labor reveals important things about us all. In my various experiences in the corporate world and in ministry, I have found that how people respond to the tasks given to them—whether they are able to complete them or not—reveals how well people know what kind of work they are suited for. Those who can complete their work effectively and efficiently have a solid grasp of what work God has called them to, and those who take too much time to complete their tasks may not yet have a strong sense of what work they are suited for. Either that, or they are simply not willing to be humble and ask for help.

Knowing what kind of work one is suited for is not the most difficult task, however, but rather knowing how to do that work effectively and efficiently in particular situations. If we cannot figure out a way to do our work more effectively and efficiently, our diligence will not serve others well. But if we know how to work effectively and efficiently at the work we are suited for, and show much dedication and discipline to complete it, our diligence is on display, and we serve others well.

But this takes time. It took me five years after planting Yullin Church to understand clearly the role of a pastor. However, I am still not sure how to efficiently and effectively execute those duties. I am still learning how to do so through time in Scripture and through conversations with my peers and mentors. This sounds like something an elementary- school student would say. But this is why I must seek wisdom from God in his Word, and prayerfully rely on both the Spirit's work in me and the insightful comments I receive from brothers and sisters in the body of Christ.

Victory in the Arena of Life

Let me end this chapter with a metaphor. Our lives are the arenas in which we work hard and sweat in order to achieve the goal of our sanctification and to give God glory in the process. This began the moment we were redeemed, and will continue until we are in heaven. As we live in this world, we come to know God's love more deeply, and to discern our duties and roles in his redemptive work. Although we are in the arena of life, we have a way out, and that way is the road of sanctification. It is a narrow road, and difficult to walk, and constantly keeps us on our toes, but it is the *only* road a Christian can take.

Of course, not everyone will travel on this road in the same way. There are some who run, some who walk, and some who go backward. There are those who carry their crosses on their shoul-ders while sweating profusely—never stopping—and there are those who pause frequently; the time they spend resting is more than the time they spend going forward. There are those who simply drop their crosses and travel however they want to, and live however they want. How would you describe how you walk this road?

If we do not lay down our laziness and take up the cross of Christ in Spirit-given faith as we walk the road of sanctification, we are bound to waste our time, and it is easy to imagine God being exasperated and frustrated at such living. There is no rest for an athlete who strives to be the best in the world. Until the race is over, the athlete's goal must be victory, and not just completion. In the same way, we are like athletes in the arena of life who should strive for victory, and not just completion. We are not meant to exist, we are meant to thrive in Christ, to live in him to the fullest (John 10:10). When the bell that signals the end of the race goes off in the arena of life, would we not want to experience the utter joy of victory—to have our hearts stirred as we embrace God, our coach and motivator? Or would we prefer loss and shame? The answer is obvious to us! But we must decide daily to keep running or to sit on the sidelines. How will you finish the day today? How will you race tomorrow?

3

The Desire for and Development of Laziness

(Proverbs 21:25)

Perversity and Palaces

Throughout history, there has been a class of mysterious people: emperors. These men lived in enormous, well-fortified, guarded palaces, while wielding absolute power and authority. Recently, I had the privilege of reading a book by a Chinese journalist that detailed the daily lives of Chinese emperors. Its contents left me fascinated.

There have been almost 600 emperors in Chinese history. Most of these emperors, apart from participating in politics, spent the majority of their time indulging in two pastimes: gluttony and lust. When most of their citizens struggled to eat two meals a day, these emperors ate four times a day. For each of their meals, much manpower and many resources were needed—from transferring the equivalent of a truckload of food to organizing the hundreds of chefs to cook each meal. These emperors made sure that only the freshest, rarest, and most precious ingredients were used for themselves and their guests. One could begin to imagine how lavish and exquisite each meal would have been, and how pitiful a peasant's meal would have been in comparison.

Yet, in spite of such a luxurious lifestyle, did the emperors live happily ever after? We might think that they did, but even though they wielded absolute power and authority, ate what they wanted to, and did whatever they pleased, most of them came to miserable ends. There were many coups and upheavals that left the imperial family in a sea of blood every time a new emperor arose. Even if certain emperors never experienced any political conflict, rarely did they live out their lives in peace and die naturally. This historical truth is not divorced from the manner in which they lived. Misery follows malevolence, and the lives of these men often epitomized the latter. They led very gluttonous, prodigal, decadent, and promiscuous lives. An example of this is seen in the life of Emperor Yang of Sui, who had hundreds of concubines—the most conservative estimate is around 400 or 500. Are there enough words to even begin to describe the promiscuity of these men?

As you might have guessed by this point in the book, laziness is behind such behavior—and laziness often rears its head in the absence of turmoil. Throughout history, when war campaigns were left behind for times of peace and prosperity—*that* is when many healthy and faithful kings abandoned all integrity and indulged in carnal desires. On this side of paradise, it seems painfully obvious that peace can be a prelude for perversity, and perversity can be linked to laziness. For example, consider a phase in the life of David. When we read about him in Scripture, we see how far someone can fall into sexual sin owing to laziness of the flesh. Here is a man after God's own heart, whose soul was decaying and groaning in the darkness after committing adultery with Uriah's wife, Bathsheba. David, if you remember, stayed at home while he sent his men away to attack the Ammonites and besiege Rabbah. Right before he was tempted, we read, "David arose from his couch and was walking on the roof of the king's house . . ." During an afternoon of rest and peace, the serpent of lust coiled around David's heart and squeezed. Carnal living, in other words, is not a luxury for the diligent. Had David been out fighting with his men, he would not have seen Bathsheba.

Preparing the Soul for Daily Living

Our position today is unique as compared to David's: while David had a clear and sufficient word from God in the Old Testament writings, today we have the completed revelation of the triune God. The Father has planned, the Son has executed, and the Spirit is applying all that God set out to do for our redemption—and it has all been written down. In other words, we have the truth of Scripture to guide us, shape us, and direct us.

We might think of the truth of Scripture as a diamond. In a dark room, a diamond seems lackluster and dull; it has a shape and texture, but we are unable to appreciate them because we are unable to see the jewel for what it is in the light. Examining the same diamond in the full light of the sun is quite a different experience. There, a rainbow of light refracts and reflects off the tiny surfaces; it radiates; it epitomizes beauty. Likewise, when we are spiritually unaware that we are in darkness, God's Word seems dull and flat. But when the light of truth shines upon our souls, when the Spirit lifts the veil of sin from our eyes, we see that God's Word is both beautiful and precious. As we meditate on it, our hearts begin to be stirred, and our lives are transformed.

This phenomenon is related to what we have been discussing in Proverbs concerning laziness. Laziness is a sort of darkness of the soul. As we meditate on the wisdom that Proverbs has to offer, we grow brighter and the world grows dimmer.

In the first chapter, if you remember, we talked about how, through the physical eye, many people appear to be busy and active. But when we look at the same people through spiritual eyes, we see that they only exert themselves to the point of exhaustion with their work, but are lazy in many other areas. This kind of spiritual laziness brings sickness of the soul until, in the end, the person is so thoroughly malnourished, so anemic, that one does not even know where to begin the healing process. This is why it is so crucial for us to always be spiritually vigilant—for the sake of our souls. We must be cognizant of the pitfalls of projecting an image to others that we are, on the one hand, lazy or, on the other hand, too busy—for both raise concerns about whether we are devoting enough time and effort to taking care of our spiritual health. The proper balance between work and rest, however, is not a matter of some sort of formula; in fact, it is as simple as leaning upon the righteousness of God: studying his Word, praying, worshiping, and trusting that he will guide us in the Spirit to do what he has planned for us to accomplish.

Think of it this way: everyone—regardless of gender, class, and ethnicity—takes the time to wash up and prepare for the day after waking up in the morning. Although some people may take longer than others to prepare, hardly anyone would start and finish the day looking as if he or she had literally rolled off the mattress and into some clothes. Even men who do not care at all about their outer appearance do the bare minimum to be well kempt. As for women, on average they seem to take about an hour to get ready—this includes washing up, getting dressed, and putting on makeup. This means that, in one year, 365 hours are spent getting ready—the equivalent of working 45 eight-hour shifts. But there are some women who do not consider this to be excessive labor. This is because everyone recognizes and does not really object to women taking as much time as they need to freshen up for their daily activities. The care and attention to detail they put into this results in our appreciating their God-given beauty, not in our chiding them for taking too long (though men are notorious for being impatient).

If this is the case, then how much time would Christians need each day to prepare their souls in order to pursue godly living? Everyone will have a different answer. But the one thing that is certain is that a lot of time will be needed—more than half a minute. Those who are spiritually mature may not need as much time to recharge their souls as others, but, on the other hand, they might be more susceptible to temptation and lust as a result. Spiritual readiness requires attention to the wardrobe described in

Ephesians 6: daily we must take up the belt of truth, the breastplate
of Christ's righteousness, the shield of faith, the sword of the Spirit,
the helmet of salvation, and the shoes of the gospel. Spiritually, we
ready ourselves not for a day at the office but for a day on the battlefield, in the presence of an enemy and his host who do not sleep.
In such a spiritual atmosphere, it is good for a mature Christian,
when he or she commits only a single sin, to be grieved more than
less mature Christians might be after committing several. But to
maintain this vigilance and sensitivity to sin, a spiritually mature
person needs time to prepare. And a spiritually immature person
will need a lot of time in order to not just realize how grievous his
sin is, but also combat it.

Excuses and Hard Questions

The issue, however, is not how much time one needs. No matter
how much time or effort one invests, or how committed one is to
recharging one's soul, the problem is the lack of preparation, the
carelessness with which we treat our daily lives. Laziness or misguided effort is inevitable if this is our habit; when we do not daily
prepare our souls for the work God has for us, we will become
spiritually lethargic or, what is perhaps more dangerous, zealous
to work for the wrong reasons. It is in this latter sense that many
have become slaves to their work, laboring from morning to night,
never even able to conceive or think about anything heavenly or do
something with gospel purpose.

But how different would it be if we daily and deeply med-
itated on Christ! We would continually receive comfort and

encouragement from the one who cares most for our souls. How different it would be if we woke up to Christ rather than to an alarm clock—if we read and prayed over the Word and looked ahead to the purposeful events and relationships God was calling us to each day!

You see, most people simply wake up to their alarm, wash up, eat breakfast, get dressed, and go to work. After work, they come back home, eat, wash up, get into their pajamas, watch television, and fall asleep. This kind of lifestyle is like that of an animal. It is impulsive, thoughtless, evoking no sense of transcendental purpose, no grand calling from the triune God of creation who upholds all things with the word of his power (Heb 1:3). It is a grave sin for someone who has received salvation and redemption to live and die like this. To do so is to throw the joy and power of our salvation in the garbage. We cannot claim Christ and carelessness at the same time. We cannot boast of a resurrected Lord and bury ourselves in work that never acknowledges his lordship. We must, in essence, learn to be busy *for God*, not busy for ourselves.

Now, it's true that we all might respond to this harsh reality with excuses: "It's not that I don't want to live a holy life; it's just that I'm already exhausted, and I don't have the time right now to figure out how to change my routine." These types of excuses suggest that preparing one's soul to be diligent—looking for ways to be renewed and empowered by grace in order to faithfully and successfully complete the calling of God on our lives—is impossible owing to the lack of time and energy.

Let's examine this sort of reasoning. There seem to be two things wrong with it. Firstly, this is essentially an expression of disobedience and a lack of desire to follow God. On the one hand, excuses related to time suggest that what God has asked us to do is not possible to accomplish in the time he has given to us. God is not being reasonable; he must change his demands or expect disappointment. Anyone with children knows that this is textbook disobedient behavior. On the other hand, excuses related to energy imply that we do not have the ability or drive to do what God has called us to do. Once again, God must change his call on our lives or settle for something less. This reflects not just disobedience, but a misplaced desire for work other than that to which God has called us. In other words, it reveals our heart's true passion, which is something other than God himself. Secondly, this leads to the possibility that a Christian could practically live without God. It implies that being a Christian does not really mean you must have a Christ-centered life, a life in which all our efforts and desires are poured into *his* mission, not ours. Anyone who is familiar with biblical teaching knows that this is patently false. To be a Christian is to be reborn (John 3); a second birth means a second life, but a life that is led only by the Spirit to do the work of Christ and his Father. Rebirth does not mean a change of opinion, as if we find the gospel more agreeable than we once did. It requires revolution: a turning of all passions and potentialities to focus on Christ and the Father's coming kingdom.

If it is plausible to hear these sorts of excuses in our head—and all of us do at some point—we need to take a good look at our-selves. If someone is not concerned with satisfying the desires of the soul even though his soul is recharged in the presence of God, is it not because he is focused more on satisfying the desires of the flesh?

These are difficult sorts of questions to ask ourselves—the sorts of questions we avoid asking—but they are necessary. If we take a moment to carefully contemplate our lives up to this point, each of us can likely remember moments of profound spiritual insight and growth, times when God opened the eyes of our hearts and burned away the fog of sin so that we could see clearly where we were and what we were supposed to do. These moments, we will find, become more frequent with an active prayer life. When we become lethargic in our attempts to commune with the triune God who called us out of darkness and into his marvelous light (1 Pet 2:9), we should not expect spiritual insight. On the other hand, if we strive to seek God through prayer every day, even the turmoil and challenges that confront us—physical trauma, broken relationships, the death of a parent—will end up leading to spiritual epiphanies, because we are more attuned to seeing the world as God sees it. Apart from communion with God, which is fostered by God's grace but also demands our continual effort, our spiritual epiphanies dwindle and disappear. All this is to say that when we offer the excuse of having too much on our plates to tend to our souls, we are actually committing ourselves to spiritual blindness.

Conversely, when we are basking in the full light of God's grace because of our longstanding efforts to commune with him, the blessing of this experience comes not because we have too much time on our hands but because we are so busy, so stretched, that we are *forced* to rely on God. Have you ever experienced the waves of God's grace in a situation such as this, where, rather than praying because you have so much time on your hands, you pray earnestly because it is your only hope? These moments reveal something critical that we often forget when difficult times pass: seeking God with all our hearts *is* our only true hope. Spiritual lethargy can take up residence in us when we believe the lie that communion with God is something we prefer rather than something we need. Just as our bodies need food to survive, our spirits need communion with God in order to thrive and grow. When we lazily resign ourselves to either not pursuing this diligently or pursuing something else with more diligence, we wilt.

The "Grace" of Get-Rich-Quick Schemes

In our incessant attempts to excuse ourselves from diligently seeking to build up our spirit through communion with God, we even turn to gambling. Ever since the lottery was introduced to Korea, there has been a "lotto craze" across the nation. The odds of actually winning, of course, are one in eight million—the same as the odds of being struck by lightning twice or getting into five car accidents in a single year. But even with these ridiculous odds, many people have illusions of winning. Thousands and thousands of people share the same hollow dream. Do they not understand how small are their chances of winning? Of course they understand; everyone knows that the lottery is a shot in the dark. So why do people play the lottery if they know that they will almost certainly not win? Perhaps one of the reasons they play is that they are sick and tired of living an honest, humble, and ordinary life; they want a change, but they know that, aside from winning the lottery, their lives will only change with sustained effort. While this is true, this seems exhausting to them, so they put their hope in a chance that change will simply come from a set of numbers selected at random. "In an instant," they think, "my life can be completely altered, my fears quieted, and my problems solved." This barren and desperate hope in sheer chance is the only version of "grace" that the world knows. While Christians put their faith in a personal God who knows and controls all things, the world puts its hope in the ancient and nebulous concept of fate.

This lottery phenomenon also occurs in our spiritual lives as Christians. We are called to deny ourselves and mortify our sins daily—over and over again. However, many Christians hate living out these implications. Instead, they hope and long for the day that God will pour out his grace and just suddenly appear, eliminating all their problems in the blink of an eye. Just as people want instant change in the physical world, in the spiritual world people would rather have transformation instantaneously than put in the constant effort and work that is required.

But do you see how the root of this desire to have everything changed in an instant, all our problems solved in the blink of an eye, is really little more than laziness? How pervasive this evil is! It's no wonder the writer of Proverbs discusses it so much. Too often people think of the biblical writers as addressing historical problems that have little contemporary relevance. Yet the relevance of biblical teaching is crystal clear when we examine our own context in the light of such teaching. Think of the patterns of behavior that are common for us in terms of physical health: failing to eat in a balanced and healthy way, refusing to push ourselves to exercise on a regular basis, turning to quick-fix solutions for weight loss and pain management—all these behaviors have the same base: lethargy. Whether it's winning the lottery or maintaining our physical health, we want immediate and easy change. The indwelling sin in us abhors sacrifice or pain of effort. This is a great evil of our time, just as it was for the writer of Proverbs.

And here is the most important part of it all: laziness is a *spiritual* evil, not just a physical one, and, sadly, it affects Christians just as much as non-Christians. There is no amount that a Christian can give, no extent of service to the church or to the world, that will present him or her with a spiritual "magic pill." There is no spiritual lottery. You cannot buy your ticket every week and cross your fingers. There is no way around it: devoting ourselves to living a holy life will mean putting into practice some uncomfortable (but biblical) words: *endurance, perseverance, diligence, patience—* the intimidating list goes on.

The Progression of Laziness—Stage 1: Not Putting Forth Our Best Effort

What exactly is laziness? It might seem odd that I have put off a definition until this point in the book, but I have been relying on our common understanding of laziness as depicted through some of the wisdom of Proverbs. We have also learned that self-love is ultimately beneath laziness. Now it is time to have a closer look at it. However, we will do so by observing the concrete consequences of laziness rather than by piecing together a definition and aiming at semantic perfection. So, in order to have a clear understanding of what laziness is, we will note how laziness progressively manifests itself. In the following paragraphs, I outline what I call the three *stages of laziness.* These stages are identified by the consequences of lazy behavior.

As I noted above, we have already looked at how the root of laziness is love of oneself. Yet this is only the cause, the initiator, of our lethargy. Moreover, self-love is not manifested as laziness apart from certain conditions. One of these conditions is that we have duties and responsibilities. If we do not have an assigned task or duty, then it is difficult to talk about our laziness, for the latter presupposes the former. No matter how devoted to ourselves we might be, we cannot be accused of laziness if we have nothing to do.

However, even if laziness can be "diagnosed" in somebody by observing what duties and responsibilities are being left by the wayside, it still seems difficult to consider laziness an evil during this first stage. But we can see that it is indeed evil when we focus more closely on our commitment to a given task. When we do not *fully* commit to a particular task, when we do not put forth our best effort, that is when the ivy of self-love begins to grow around our hearts. However, in the secular world, many people do not believe that not fully committing ourselves to completing a duty or task is a serious evil. That is why this first stage of laziness can easily go unnoticed. But, make no mistake, it is certainly there. Stage 1 of laziness is simply giving less than 100 percent or being careless and reckless in completing a task. In other words, at this stage, we have not blatantly refused to do something; rather, we have made a decision to *not* put forth our best effort.

So why would we not want to put forth our best effort? The simple answer is that to do so would require expending strength and energy, which, for one reason or another, we don't want to expend. Perhaps it's because we are not interested in or passionate about something, or we feel that the payoff isn't worth it, or we have a selfish desire to expend energy on something self-gratifying. Whatever the particular reason is, it seems to be enough to convince us that we shouldn't put in our best effort. But, once we make that decision, we make another underlying decision to ignore the purpose for which we were made. As image-bearers of the triune God, we were made to reflect him, and the triune God never stops working. Recall Jesus's words in the New Testament when he was criticized for healing a man on the Sabbath: "My Father is working until now, and I am working" (John 5:17). The Father always works, so the Son always works, and we can easily infer that the Spirit is always working, since the Word of God that was given through him is ever "living and active" (Heb 4:12). God always works; he has no need of rest.

We, on the other hand, do need to rest, but our rest is meant to help us recover strength so that we can continue to put forth our best effort in all that we do, for God's glory. In other words, we were created to give our best in everything—no matter how difficult our situation might be. When we choose not to do so, we choose at the same time to act against the image we carry as God's creatures. We must, as far as we are able, follow Christ and work as long as we see our heavenly Father working. This will be a witness to the watching world, for those who ignore Christ and the message of the gospel see no problem in putting in only half the effort. Because they refuse to accept what God has done for them in Christ, they also refuse to live as Christ lived.

Failing to put in our best effort also reveals that God is not at the center of our life; instead, some other desire is controlling us. This is the very definition of idolatry, and yet we seldom think of it that way. Being lazy is less offensive than being idolatrous, so we will put up with the former critique and do what we can to avoid the latter. Yet ignoring something does not mean it goes away. A lazy heart *is* an idolatrous heart, and such a heart cannot be in harmony with God. When we are out of harmony with God, things become worse, and that leads us to stage 2 in the progression of laziness.

The Progression of Laziness—Stage 2: Abandoning Duties and Responsibilities

If laziness is not addressed at stage 1, then it quickly advances to stage 2. In this stage, we abandon our duties and responsibilities. This is nothing surprising, for laziness is only restrained by the will, and when we are lazy, having a weak or apathetic will is the problem in the first place. At the heart of laziness, however, is not simply the will. As we discussed earlier, laziness is ultimately rooted in self-love, and self-love only spreads and grows stronger as we neglect it. Give a wicked heart an inch, and it will take a mile. Self-love grows so strong so quickly because it is the potent core of sinful behavior. In effect, self-love is the desire for self-governance; it is our desire to supplant God and be our own masters. In other words, it is the desire to become like God. In Reformed circles, this is commonly labeled "autonomy," and this was the cause of the very first sin: in rejecting God's Word and listening to the lies of the serpent, Adam and Eve expressed their desire to become "like God" (Gen 3:5). John Frame reminds us that this desire, this spirit of autonomy, can be seen in all sin.[1] Autonomy, then, is linked to laziness in an important way: the desire for self-governance is closely tied to our self-love.

Given the threat that autonomy and self-love pose to our spiritual health, it is tragic that so many people today do not see laziness as a big problem. They would be surprised to hear us speak of laziness as related to what some Reformed theologians consider the most dangerous sin we can commit. Perhaps that is part of what makes laziness so deadly: it is a spiritual assassin that lives in the home of every human heart, but we treat it as a common thief who drops into our lives occasionally and steals something unnoticeable. Such an illustration reminds us why so many people are ignorant of laziness even as they are being ruined by it.

We might draw out this illustration a bit further. When we look at history, we quickly find that many kings were killed by knife-wielding assassins. However, this was not the only method. In fact, the best way to assassinate kings was to poison their food and kill them slowly. The official records of many nations reveal that the latter method was used more frequently. Assassins that embraced this method of attack were successful if they went *undetected*. So, while we often think of spiritually fatal sins such as murder, adultery, lies, and apostasy as knife-wielding spiritual assassins, we must guard ourselves against another, quieter assassin who seeks to poison and thus slowly kill us: laziness. That is precisely why we have said that spiritual vigilance is not merely a virtue; it is necessary if we are to maintain our spiritual vitality. If we are caught off

---

1 John M. Frame, *The Doctrine of the Word of God* (Phillipsburg, NJ: P&R, 2010), 16.

guard for even a moment, we might miss the poison that was put in our food.

So if the first stage of the manifestation of laziness is half-heartedly completing our duties, then the next stage is quitting our duties altogether. The *manner* in which we act is bound to the *matter* of our action; when we begin to put forward something less than our best effort, it may only be a matter of time before we put in no effort at all. We must mark, then, not just what we do each day, but how we do it. It is a short distance, in other words, from stage 1 of laziness to stage 2. The depletion of effort often leads to its abandonment. Working half-heartedly leads to not working at all. However, laziness does not end here.

The Progression of Laziness—Stage 3: Carnal Passions

Laziness is not content with living a comfortable life, with merely doing nothing. In fact, in comparison to its main goal, living a comfortable life is fairly minor. Once someone is content after achieving this minor goal, once someone has lived in stage 2 for long enough, the main goal is in sight: absolute pleasure. And just as laziness often goes unchecked (since our desire for self-love grows stronger) and has no end in sight, so there is no end to chasing after absolute pleasure. It is the spiritual equivalent of falling off a cliff—there is nothing to stop the plunge of our soul but the hard ground of God's righteousness.

Remember, I speak here of Christians, not merely people in general. A believer who does his good and proper duties only half-heartedly will, in the end, gain and acquire comfort, but ruin his relationship with God. The godly joy that results from the unity forged by love flowing from harmonious relations with the triune God—that joy first fractures, then fades, and finally disappears. At this point, laziness will not give our flesh any peace or contentment, but will demand more stimulation and pleasure. Much of the time, that demand cannot be satisfied without sinning in some way. Indeed, the demand itself is sinful and idolatrous, since it longs for something other than communion with God.

Now, there is variety in the different desires or demands that flow out of a person, but there is even greater variety in how those desires and demands are addressed. All humans are born with fallen, carnal desires and demands, but these were not predestined to control us. Once the seed of grace has been planted in the soil of our hearts by the Holy Spirit, we begin to experience new desires and demands—those fitting of a restored soul that is destined to conform to the image of God's Son (Rom 8:29). Because God's grace cannot be resisted or restrained, divine desires and demands take the reins of our life, and the evil or allegedly "instinctual" desires of the sinful self become more anemic. Of course, there is backward and forward movement in our journey of sanctification, but the ultimate direction is already decided, and the progress is sure. For those of us reborn in Christ, the desires of the soul that mark our identity begin to resemble holy desires.

This is important to remember because it can be easy to keep our true desires hidden by committing righteous actions. But we know that God looks at the heart and soul (1 Sam 16:7). "This is important to remember because it can be easy to keep our true desires hidden by committing righteous actions. But we know that God looks at the heart and soul (1 Sam 16:7). The Puritan John Owen once remarked, 'He (God) doth it to show unto man what is in him,—that is, the man himself; and that either as to his grace or to his corruption ... Grace and corruption lie deep in the heart... .'"[2]

But, unfortunately, even though we know this, laziness still encourages us to suppress what we know to be true. As Christians, we know that God looks at the heart and sees what is done in secret (Matt 6:4, 18), and yet we constantly live as if he does not. But it does not stop there. We do not end with merely a façade of righteousness; rather, our spirits grow sicker and more anemic as we give ourselves over to carnal passions. The ultimate goal of laziness, remember, is to cause a person to be consumed by carnality, to live purely according to the flesh. We see once more that laziness is not simply a bad habit; it has grand schemes that Satan himself wants to impose on us.

Thus, with advanced laziness (stage 3), carnal desires flow abundantly throughout the believer's heart; we are no longer content with mere comfort. Instead, we become restless and are prodded to commit evil actions that we know, in the seat of our souls, are contrary to who we are in Christ. In the early stages of laziness, we are comfortable as long as Scripture does not require us to *do* something, but as laziness progresses, we actually find that we are, in fact, working: we are spending ourselves pursuing anything that gives us pleasure—even sin. So a paradox emerges in our personal lives: we tell ourselves that we don't want to work, but then we end

---

2 John Owen, *The Works of John Owen*, vol. 6, *On Temptation* (Edinburgh: The Banner of Truth Trust, 1991), 93.

up working very hard to get what we should not have. Moreover, this latter desire for evil is stronger than the former desire (the desire to do nothing). This is because the toll we pay, the pain the psyche and soul endure, in resisting and fighting the urge to commit sin is greater than that of simply refusing to act.

Think of it this way: what would happen if red, bloody meat were placed outside the cage of a lion that had not eaten for days? It would lose itself in longing—salivating, wailing, roaring. Leaving food for the lion to eat when it is unable to satisfy its desire will take a much greater psychological toll on the lion than if it was simply hunting and chasing elusive prey in the wild. If we learn anything from stage 3 of laziness, let it be this: laziness is far more dangerous than we think it will be when we begin doing something half-heartedly. Its goal is the soul's destruction, and it achieves this by turning our initial impressions of laziness on their head: we think laziness is about doing too little, but it ends up being about doing too much— too much of the flesh and not enough (if any) of the spirit.

The Comparative Growth of Laziness

Still, even with all that we can learn from these three stages of laziness, perhaps the simplest way to reveal the growth of laziness is by thinking of it comparatively: how do we move from being somewhat lazy but mostly active to being very lazy and almost inactive (spiritually and physically)? Laziness often surfaces in the form of questions such as, "Do I really have to do that? What's the point of doing it that way? Do most people even go through this much trouble? Am I still expected to follow through on this even though

I'm an infant in the faith?" The more these questions are answered in ways that give laziness a foothold, the more quickly we sink into physical and spiritual lethargy. As we give in to the desires of the flesh, our desire to fight laziness in our hearts is extinguished. Whether we think of laziness in terms of the three stages or in terms of our comparative inactivity, the point is that we seldom move from being completely active to being completely inactive. Lethargy is something that grows, and that is why we are called to be vigilant with regard to its presence in our lives.

Sometimes, developing this vigilance and awareness comes about by our engagement with others who live differently from us. When we observe how other people live, this can show us not only how they respond to the threat of laziness but also how we can respond to that same threat in ways we might not have considered. For instance, I am an ordained minister, but I tend to live with the mentality of a layperson—an average churchgoer —rather than that of a minister. I do this not because I am trying to forget the duties and responsibilities of a pastor, but rather because I believe that someone who is not aware of the duties and responsibilities of a layperson will certainly be unaware of the duties and responsibilities that come with shepherding such people. Looking at the lives of others helps me to examine my own life and to maintain vigilance and awareness of what I am called to do.

To some people, this might seem strange. Why take lessons from those whom we are meant to teach and shepherd? Is there not some sort of distinction among believers that leads to differing responsibilities? Surely, but this does not mean that we dichotomize classes of believers and ignore the mutual dependence of members in the body of Christ. To a certain degree, something similar to this can be seen in the Catholic tradition. Catholics have traditionally recognized two classes of believers: those who teach (clergy) and those who learn (laity). Those who taught were supposed to teach the laity well, while those who learned were supposed to listen well. The New Testament, however, does not make such a sharp division between these two groups of believers. While there is order in the body of Christ, we all have equal standing before God, and are one body attached to the Head, Jesus Christ. We are also God's children, and at the same time, are called to live our lives fully and with great effort before God. This means that teachers and pastors learn a great deal from taking on the mentality, the perspective, of those whom they serve. In fact, doing so can help pastors to serve their flocks with greater diligence because we then become more aware of the needs of our people.

Of course, there is a negative counterpart to this. There are people who justify their belief that not everyone is part of the mutually interdependent body in Christ. Sometimes we ourselves can act this way. We may have less of a pull from our conscience concerning our abandonment of certain duties or our tendency to organize our faith according to selfish agendas and worldly values, the latter of which are weeds that need to be pulled from the garden of our ever-maturing faith. We also might compare ourselves to others and assume that we are better than they are, since, perhaps, we pray or read Scripture more consistently than we think they do. This attitude of superiority is sinful and always leads to pride of one sort or another.

Contrast these negative behaviors with the grace we experience in Christ. Grace fills us with God's love and sanctifies us. It turns us away from ourselves and toward the needs of those around us. This is mainly because when we focus exclusively on the love we have for God and the love he has for us, we truly appreciate and become overwhelmed by this love—so much so that pride, jealously, and our subjective comparisons begin to seem petty (because they *are* petty). When the love of God becomes our standard for all of life, we view things through his eyes, not through the eyes of another sinful person. Through God's eyes (the God who gave his Son to die on the cross and raised him by the Spirit on our behalf), we can look at the lives of others in a sanctified way, learning how we can more diligently serve the God who served us by taking up godly responsibilities in the body of Christ. In short, God's love fills us with joy and contentment so that we can labor to the joy and contentment of others. This is why 1 Corinthians 13:4 reminds us that love does not envy. Why does it not envy? Because God's love is the object of joy, and when we focus on that object, we will want to image the God who is always working for our good. Envy is the fruit of discontentment, and no heart that truly discovers the love of God for us in Christ will respond with envy or jealousy, since those feelings are the marks of discontentment.

This same principle applies to the believer's awareness of his action, of the way in which he lives his life. When our faith is full, we are not concerned about other people's attitudes or standards. The only thing we are concerned about is this: "What kind of believer does the Bible call me to be? How does God want me to live my life?" Only God's thoughts and standards should be the compass that directs our conscience and faith, and only God's holy love can free us from the comparative growth of laziness and the sin of superiority.

The Sprouts of Laziness Are Growing

Without God's holy love (or, if we become negligent of that love), our spiritual vigor is reduced and we are made less content. It is at that moment—the moment when we fail to be content with the holy love of God in Christ—that laziness begins to advance and take control of us, eventually leading us to be governed by carnal desires. And a profound danger lies here, in that our witness is undermined. If, by the course of laziness, we are consumed by carnal desires, then no one can see us as people living under the rule of God's grace anymore. We then appear to live under the rule of sin and to have become its slaves. Spiritually, we invert the truth of Romans 6:17 and resemble those who do not know Christ. If this is the destination to which laziness wants to lead us, we must realize that it will not stop until it accomplishes its goal, and so we must be vigilant in guarding against its advances.

In light of this, if we do not want this miserable fate to be realized in our lives, we must take preemptive measures to eradicate laziness. If we want to ensure that laziness does not penetrate and dwell in us, we must remember from the outset that living according to Scripture will require much commitment and dedication; this will mean *daily* attention to what God has called us to do. A practical way to begin implementing this sort of lifestyle is to spend daily time in God's Word and in prayer. This helps to cultivate our reliance on God's strength and our prioritization of his will for us on a regular basis. Giving God the top priority in our lives, however, will mean that we commit to a lifestyle of self-denial, for living such a life is the best way to keep the seeds of laziness from taking root.

Of course, this may cause us to ask ourselves, "How long do I have to live like this? Is there a time when I will find rest from such hard work? Won't living like this place extra stress on us and even lead us to lose our joy because we are so focused on diligence?" These are important questions to answer. But before we answer them, we must remind ourselves of the biblical worldview that we have undertaken. Work is not meant to be wearisome, nor is it meant to bleed us dry of joy. Rather, work is meant to be fulfilling, to lead us to happiness and a deeper, more fulfilling sense of joy. We saw how, in the garden of Eden, work was part of Adam and Eve's calling; they were created as image-bearing workers. Surely, they rested from their labors (and God modeled this for them by resting on the seventh day), but such rest was not meant to be a refuge from joyless work; it was meant to rejuvenate them, so that they would arise and happily image God once more. This is important in the context of the questions we have just asked. Living faithfully and diligently, while it involves self-sacrifice, is the key to living with genuine happiness. This is because God is not only concerned with the results of labor; he enjoys the labor itself. In creation, God labored for six days—sin had not entered the picture yet. So we can infer that such labor was wholly *good*, and the triune God enjoyed doing it. God has not called us to a diligent life because he wants to crush our spirits or sap all our energy. Instead, he has called us to live diligently because doing so faithfully images him. In fact, as we strive to image God faithfully, we will find that his desire is to compensate us for this arduous process. Just consider the passages in Matthew 6 that reference "rewards" for those who live as diligent and godly servants:

> But when you give to the needy, do not let your left hand know what your right hand is doing, so that your giving may be in secret. And your Father who sees in secret will reward you. (Matt 6:3–4)

> But when you pray, go into your room and shut the door and pray to your Father who is in secret. And your Father who sees in secret will reward you. (Matt 6:6)

> But when you fast, anoint your head and wash your face, that your fasting may not be seen by others but by your Father who is in secret. And your Father who sees in secret will reward you. (Matt 6:17–18)

Meditating on these truths may help us view work in a whole new light. Yet, even with this knowledge, we often find ourselves becoming negative about living diligently and find ourselves not fully committing ourselves to our duties. When we notice this happening, we are called to repent. This is part of what it means to be vigilant regarding our laziness, for even though negativity in itself is not laziness, if it is left alone, it will quickly lead to stage 1 (and then on to stages 2 and 3). Negativity (complaining, discontentment, cynicism), in this sense, is a sign that we are not content with the work God has called us to, and, if we give up on that work, we will not find ourselves free of all responsibilities; as we have seen, we will simply replace godly work with sinful work as we strive after desires of the flesh. The peace and joy we had in doing God's work will be replaced by discontentment and irritation by the world's sinful desires, which swarm around our ears like bees. They will not leave us alone, because Satan knows that we must be filled with something—be it God's desires or those of the world. There is no compromise between the two. Either we work for God or we work for something else (see Matt 6:24). In this sense, we must be vigilant so that we do not compromise with laziness.

The gravity of our vigilance might be expressed with an illustration. To compromise with laziness and let its seeds take root in our lives is like a swallow building a nest. As she builds her nest, she weaves in bits of poisonous fibers from a nearby factory, along with leaves and twigs that have been contaminated by pollutants. Without changing the material from which her nest is built, the nest becomes more dangerous for the eggs that she has laid there and for herself. If the swallow thinks, "Ah, yes—I'll begin building a new nest tomorrow," but then never follows through with her intention and ignores what she knows to be harmful, then she only exacerbates the situation. At some point, she will need to leave and build a new nest from clean material. Likewise, we cannot allow the seeds of laziness to sit in the soil of our heart, ignoring them simply because of their small size. We cannot put vigilance off until tomorrow, nor can we allow momentary success—a spell of diligent labor—to blind us to impending threats. When we seem to be conquering laziness, it can be easy to adopt an attitude of care-lessness when laziness begins to enter our lives again. We might think, "I've been working hard; I descrve to be a little lazy; I'll just wait a little longer until I'm ready to get back into a lifestyle of diligence." Such thinking does not lead to rest; it merely waters the seeds of lethargy and then gives them time to grow stronger.

Brothers and sisters, we simply cannot live like this. No amount of piety or spiritual vigor or passion for theology can replace our need to remain diligent. We can shed tears at the thought of God's beautiful love, but it means nothing if we do not respond to such love by pouring ourselves out in living response to the triune God who finds joy in labor. Being busy for God, in other words, is part of practicing our faith. We will never really attain the biblical virtues we hold so dearly if we do not practice our faith through dedicated, God-centered diligence.

What's more, when we do not put our faith into practice, we begin to lose our freedom and confidence—two critical weapons in the great spiritual war that we have been born into. While those who go to work early in the morning and labor steadfastly are con-fident in any circumstance, those in whom laziness is prone to blossom spend the majority of their time being concerned about the opinions of others; the absence of work in their own lives turns the labor of those around them into threats to their security, and these threats then make them self-conscious of what *those* peo-ple think, rather than mindful of what *God* thinks. And God sees far more than our coworkers (see Matt 6); he sees in secret. The life that God expects from us is one in which we can boldly and unashamedly show that we are his children who faithfully commit and dedicate ourselves to the work that he has providentially given to us, and we make the necessary sacrifices to fulfill our roles. That life is all that he wants for us. It is a simple life, but it is also a life of joy, a life of faithfully imaging the God of Scripture.

The Pattern of Jesus's Life

Since we desire to faithfully image the God of the Bible, now would be a fitting time to turn our attention to the Son of God himself.

When we are genuinely putting in the effort to live a life of focused diligence, a life that breaks off from the desires of laziness, and to complete our duties, we will undoubtedly encounter resistance from evil, so much so that we might find ourselves in tears as we pray in desperation, "God, please help me!" But, regrettably, there are not many instances when we have lived this way, are there? Let us take a moment to think about when Jesus was praying in the garden of Gethsemane. If you remember the passage, it tells us that he was praying so hard and was so exhausted that drops of blood fell from his brow, but God sent angels to strengthen him (Luke 22:43). In this striking account—an account that shows not only how much pressure Christ was under but also how committed he was to his Father's mission—we are given a paradigm for our own struggle to carry out God's will for our lives. Notice that God sent his angels to Christ in Christ's moment of *need*. God is always faithful to do so. Yet, when we live with relative ease and comfort, it is difficult to expect God to move and work in our lives; in fact, we might even wonder whether God needs to work in our lives, since we seem to be doing so well "on our own." But when laziness leads us to live relatively comfortable and selfish lives, it also keeps us from receiving God's help and conquers us in our spiritual struggle—by suggesting that we should avoid struggle at all costs!

When we feel like compromising with laziness, we must think of our Lord. When we look at the course of his short life on earth, can we detect any traces of laziness? Do we read of any occurrence in Scripture where he neglected or abandoned his duties, or was consumed by his desires? No. And notice what we *do* see in Scripture: God endlessly poured out upon his Son the Holy Spirit, and gave him the power to exorcise demons and raise the dead with a single word. And yet, because he was modeling true sonship for us, Jesus never once relied on his own power and sovereignty when he was serving us. Instead, he leaned on God the Father every second that he spent on earth. Although he did not sin, he still had all the physical weaknesses and was truly human. So it would have been a lot easier for him to simply stay put, lie down, and rest all the time instead of traveling everywhere and preaching. Rather than enduring the persecution and insults of those who did not recognize his lordship, he would have had an easier life if he had simply rested in all the hospitality and compliments and gifts of those who loved him. But Jesus firmly refused all of that because he had a mission from God and duties that he had to fulfill. That is why he preached to others and healed the sick, and prayerfully lived life with all his effort and energy—even until the end, when he offered up his body and bled for us.

In contrast, look at how the world is today. Many people are still unaware and ignorant of the gospel, and those who say they have heard and know the gospel do not obey it or live faithfully according to its call. How then can we live as people who have received the light of truth in a world where apostate-like faith is so pervasive?

Certainly, this will not be easy. But not once did Jesus ever say that the road of a disciple is easy. On the contrary, he showed personally that that road will demand your life—all that you have. That is what our ancestors in the faith always knew they were risking in taking this "road of faith." That, in fact, is why the faith was able to spread so rapidly—owing to their absolute loyalty even in the face of death and their willingness to give up their lives for the sake of God's work.

God's Help Is Greater Than We Could Ever Imagine

A young man came to me one day, seeking my help. He was working endlessly, and as we were talking, I encouraged him to develop a prayer life. With a gloomy and sullen countenance, he said, "Pastor, if I wake up early to pray at this point in my life, I will break down and lose it." Because he seemed to have already made up his mind to not have devotional time in the morning, I ended our session and parted ways with him. But, soon after, he came to me again. He shared that my insistence that he pray had weighed heavily on his heart, and he had decided to attend regular morning prayer services. He then said, "Pastor, there is something that I can't help but acknowledge. I thought that waking up earlier than

I normally do would only make me more tired and miserable. But by overcoming that concern and coming before God every morning, I never imagined that God would give me new strength."

God works and moves in ways that utterly surpass our expectations, as he did with this young man. Also, because we believe in this God, we can dive headlong into situations and projects that human calculations and perceptions cannot account for.

Beloved reader, I pray that you and I would rid ourselves of laziness and live faithfully and diligently. If we decide to live that kind of life, God will surely help. No matter how difficult and bitter the pain and endurance that must be paid in order to cultivate diligence, it is nothing compared to the pain that our souls would endure by being swallowed up by our desires in lazy living. When do we start? Well, even if we are struggling with lethargy right now, the easiest way to defeat it is to immediately dust ourselves off, stand up, roll up our sleeves, and put into practice what we know thus far about living a diligent life. After learning about the identity and route of laziness, there is no better time to defeat it than right now. The more one pushes off fighting against laziness, the harder the fight will become. Laziness is a great enemy that does not rest. And we must remember that it leads us not to another road, but to the cliff of carnal passions, where we exchange work for a holy God for work for a fallen world.

4

The Carelessness
of Laziness
(Proverbs 24:30-31)

Losing a Job Because of One Word

At one point in the history of a certain company, the accounting department was working frantically to prepare the documents for a very large construction project. A notice to alert potential bidders for the project went out to the papers, and, as usual, many bidders sent in their deposits the day before the bidding in the hope that they would secure the contract. Out of all the deposits (usually a tenth of the total cost of the construction) that were sent, the cheapest one was to be chosen. Everything was proceeding according to the typical rules, but as strict evaluations of the submitted bids were being carried out, a big commotion arose. For some reason, many bidders came with their deposits on the day of the bidding, instead of submitting them the day before. They demanded that they be allowed to bid for the contract as well. What had happened?

It was later found out that the notice originally sent to the newspapers had the following intended message: "Any companies that desire to bid for this project should send a deposit that is equal to a tenth of their estimated cost the day *before* the actual bidding." However, the newspapers made a typo. The message they had printed ended with ". . . the day *of* the actual bidding." The person in charge of the company's accounting department received disciplinary action, while the person who rushed and misprinted the announcement in the newspaper lost his job—all over a single word.

Most people would not consider the actions of this person to be lazy—rushing to print the notice in the newspapers and then making a careless error. But in that small and significant moment of carelessness, there were hints of laziness, for he did not want to waste any more time, effort, or energy going over and double-checking his work for mistakes. He wanted to conserve his energy, and thought that wasting more time on his task would be fruitless. It turns out that it wouldn't have been fruitless; it would have allowed him to keep his job. Neglecting a detail because of laziness can have disastrous consequences. While we learn this from our daily experience, we also can see it taught in the pages of Scripture. The Bible considers negligence to be the result of laziness. This is what we will explore in this chapter.

Wisdom That Values Time

Even if we say that we live in fear of God, we all need guidance and the desire to gain wisdom in order to live capably in God's presence and to not waste our lives. It's true that the spiritual change in someone who moves from being in Adam to being in Christ (see Rom 5:12–21; 1 Cor 15:22) is difficult. Such a change requires rebirth (John 3), which means a comprehensive transformation in thought and action. However, sometimes this seems easy in comparison to the change that must take place in order for diligence to replace laziness in the Christian life. A person on fire for the Lord needs to acquire concrete methods that will allow him to be devoted and faithful to the Lord, and this is a domain that demands wisdom. Thankfully, God has provided this wisdom in his Word.

Truthfully, the transformation of our souls and the change in our disposition that results from salvation is something all people should strive for and desire. Before coming to Christ, we had hearts of stone, and we needed spiritual surgery so that God could give us a heart of flesh and a new spirit (Ezek 36:26). However, God is not content with this alone, for he desires not just the heart, but our entire life to be an expression and confession of his holy love. Therefore, behind a believer's emotions and feelings of love for God must certainly be thoughts such as, "How can I live my life in a way that proves my love for God with the short amount of time I have?"

On the one hand, when we discover the truth of the gospel in Scripture, we experience ineffable joy. On the other hand, unimaginable regret and pain might attack our hearts for subsequent months and years. Why? Because we realize not only what we now have in Christ but also what we had given up while we were rejecting him. For years, we might have struggled with a sinful habit that prevented any sort of spiritual growth, repeatedly slipping and falling down a rocky hill that was covered in wet moss. But I truly believe that the simple truth of the gospel removes us from these places: through the Word, the Spirit shows us a way to break the vicious cycle that had made us spiritually stagnant. When I think back on the moments when I was trapped in a vicious cycle, I feel much regret, which pains me greatly, for if someone had taught me the truth of the gospel earlier, I would not have wasted my life and time.

I heard a similar testimony from a minister whom I studied with after attending an event in the US. He told me that if he had read a book I had written—*Are You Really Walking Down That Road?*—twenty years earlier, he could have saved ten years and had a more effective ministry.

Perhaps some of this regret might be avoided if we did not so strictly divorce time and money. If a close friend were to ask you to borrow $1,000, you might try to find an excuse not to lend him the money. Yet we are very accommodating and generous to a stranger who asks us to give him our time. This is a tragic mistake, for money can be earned back again, but time can never be regained.

Time is a precious gift. Both those who are generally diligent and those who struggle with laziness have the same twenty-four-hour day. However, the former have a passion to bring glory to God and thus think not only about the hours but about the minutes and the seconds—every segment of time is like a piece of gold because every segment of time is an opportunity to spread God's glory.

As I hope to have made plain by now, the truths that can be gleaned from the wisdom in Proverbs are more than enough to make our lives more fruitful and efficient, to make us see how precious time is. It follows, then, that if we take the time to extract and familiarize ourselves with these truths, the value that it adds to our spiritual life is immeasurable.

A Land That Is Ruined

In this chapter, we will take a look at Proverbs 24:30–31:

> I passed by the field of a sluggard,
>> by the vineyard of a man lacking sense,
> and behold, it was all overgrown with thorns;
>> the ground was covered with nettles,
>> and its stone wall was broken down.

The author of this proverb wanted to share his observations with us. One time, he passed by the field and vineyard of a sluggard who lacked common sense. He noticed that there were thorns everywhere, the ground was covered with weeds, and the stone wall was in ruins. What this man planted in his field we will never know, but, whatever it was, it would not have been very fruitful. What we do know from this text, however, is that this field and the vineyard were not unused and abandoned; they had crops planted in them. If there were not, the verse would have said "an abandoned field" rather than "the field of a sluggard, . . . the vineyard of a man lacking sense." So, even though we don't know what kind of field it was, we at least know there was some sort of grain growing, and there were grapevines as well. For the Israelites, grain was their staple food, and grapes were used to make wine, which they drank more than water. That is why this field and vineyard, even in the hands of a lazy owner, were not just left uncultivated. The land was absolutely necessary for survival. If it did not yield crops or produce a harvest, the people would be in dire straits.

The Danger of Using Weakness as an Excuse

So this field and vineyard that are absolutely critical for survival have weeds growing in them. There are thorns and thistles, as well as a crumbling stone wall. How did it get to this point? Did the owner of the land go out and sow seeds of thorns, thistles, and weeds? Did he take a hammer and demolish his own wall to allow animals and trespassers easy access? Of course not. And yet the blame still falls on the owner.

Now, there may be a good reason why the land is the way it is—perhaps the owner became ill or his workers abandoned him, or maybe his age prevented him from laboring intensely. But, whatever the reason, we might be suspicious if the owner turned out to be a young, healthy man who then tried to justify himself by saying that he was too weak. Why would our suspicions be raised? Well, in our time, we are ordinarily lax when it comes to using weakness as an excuse to not carry out our duties. But, as we can confirm by our personal experiences, this is more often because we are lazy, not really because we lack the strength. People who are really weak are not derelict in their duties, and do not hide behind the excuse of weakness or fragility.

A weak and fragile person confesses to the Lord that he is nothing and thinks that he can do nothing without the Lord. This, we would all agree, is a biblical way to live. Consider the following poem by the German poet Rainer Maria Rilke, "Day in Autumn":

> After the summer's yield, Lord, it is time
> to let your shadow lengthen on the sundials
> and in the pastures let the rough winds fly.
>
> As for the final fruits, coax them to roundness.
> Direct on them two days of warmer light
> to hale them golden toward their term, and harry
> the last few drops of sweetness through the wine.
>
> Whoever's homeless now will build no shelter;
> who lives alone will live indefinitely so,
> waking up to read a little, draft long letters,
> and, along the city's avenues,
> fitfully wander, when the wild leaves loosen.[1]

We might imagine Rilke thinking the following thoughts as he wrote: "Although farmers have planted the seed, weeded, fertilized, and watered the field, it is not by their work and strength that the land yields its fruit. Lord, please give two more days of southern light, and allow these grapes to ripen." The truly weak and fragile

---

1 Rainer Maria Rilke, "Day in Autumn," trans. Mary Kinzie, *Poetry*, April 2008, http://www.poetryfoundation.org/poetrymagazine/poems/detail/50937.

person is the one who has this attitude in the depths of his heart, the one who knows that only God brings growth (see 1 Cor 3:7). This sense of weakness is biblically warranted and should be in the hearts of both those who are physically strong and those who are physically weak.

Yet there is another sense of weakness—a worldly, sinful sense. According to this sense, weakness is used not to reflect the soul's disposition before an all-powerful God but to sidestep responsibility. Such claims of weakness are shameful because they are really just laziness in disguise. We may not want to acknowledge this and may choose instead to mask our lethargy with a claim of fragility, but in our hearts we know our motives, as does the God who sees in secret (Matt 6). Laziness brings out the worst in us. It not only makes us unproductive, it also encourages us to lie and cheat in order to avoid labor.

Take a practical example, such as prayer. When we cannot be faithful and consistent in the discipline of prayer, it is usually not because of weakness, though we might claim that this is a valid excuse because of the difficulty we encounter in focusing. Rather, it is all too often linked to laziness, a refusal to make a sustained effort in communing with God. Not to pray, in fact, is quite easy because it requires almost no effort. If we want to know how to *not* pray, we do not need to read a book or study different methods to avoid prayer. We simply stop thinking about it and turn our attention elsewhere. To learn how to cultivate an active prayer life, on the other hand, can be a lot of work for us, and it will mean sacrifice—perhaps waking up earlier or choosing to pray instead of going to the gym. Whatever the sacrifices might be, the work that a diligent prayer life requires is too often enough to keep us from cultivating one.

But notice how this is an issue of choice. The same applies to our practice of reading Scripture. When we give up spending time in God's Word and wrestling with its implications for our lives, have we really made this decision out of weakness, because we are not mentally or physically able to read, or have we simply chosen to elevate other desires and activities above God's Word? We know all too well that the latter is the driving cause. Choice, more often than weakness, is what directs our path.

When we are tempted to bring up weakness before God in order to suggest that we had no choice in making some decision, we might better discern our spiritual posture if we ask ourselves a couple of questions: "Did God force me into making this decision, or was there another way (a way that perhaps required more work)? Did I make this mistake because I was bound to or because I was careless?" Such simple questions, when answered candidly, will usually reveal what is really going on in our hearts.

When we avoid such questions, we are potentially adding hypocrisy to the sin of laziness, and that makes laziness all the more sinister and all the more difficult to forgive. For some people, witnessing laziness in others makes their blood boil. And yet, there are not many people who seem to ask forgiveness for their laziness. Instead, they ask forgiveness for their deceit, which is undergirded by laziness! Moreover, because most people do not consider laziness a deadly evil, many will not consider it an enemy—even though it wages war against our souls, and even though, as we have seen, its final aim is to turn us over to carnal desires.

Laziness and Being Incomplete

Let us return to the sluggard and his field. The field and the vineyard were ruined because the one responsible for their cultivation
and care was careless. The owner, instead of faithfully carrying out
his duty, did nothing, which led to the ruin of the field and the
vineyard. Note how this confirms what we have already found: destruction can come from laziness just as easily as it can come from
fire. In a sense, the sluggard might as well have lit his field on fire,
for his actions were achieving the same result in the end, even if to
a lesser degree.

The proverb here also draws our attention to the descriptors of
this person. The writer calls the owner of this field and vineyard "a
sluggard" and "a man lacking sense." The author could have talked
about the field and the vineyard without mentioning the owner,
or he could have looked at both pieces of land and explained the
condition of each piece according to the specific personality of the
owner, as is sometimes done in Hebrew poetry. But, for whatever
reason, that is not the important issue. The problem here is that
the field and the vineyard are not suffering from different circumstances, but from the same circumstance. Effectively, the author
employs the identifiers "a sluggard" and "a man lacking sense" because he considers them the same.

In the original language, the word that is translated as "sluggard" is slightly closer in meaning to a more derogatory expression, such as "lazy, good-for-nothing fool." The phrase that is
translated as "a man lacking sense" in the original Hebrew actually
means someone with an incomplete heart. The word for wisdom

is usually *hōchma*, but in this verse the word used is *lev*, which actually means "heart." When one considers how *lev* is usually translated in Scripture, it tends to be used and understood in the context of "understanding" or "differentiating." So, if we were to follow the nuances of the Hebrew, we could understand this verse as describing "the field of a sluggard, . . . the vineyard of someone whose heart is incomplete." An incomplete heart may, in this sense, refer to someone who has not given himself wholly to the God who is always working. What's worse, this incomplete heart is also a heart that lacks wisdom, which is usually given by God to those who are doing their best for his glory. Solomon's prayer (2 Chr 1; 1 Kgs 3) is a good example of this.

Wisdom Given to the One Who Does His Best

We find more confirmation that God gives wisdom to those who put forth their best efforts in the following story about an evangelist in China. At one time, China was free and open to missions, so a certain evangelist was able to lead his fellow workers to proclaim the gospel above ground across the continent. Everywhere he went, hundreds or thousands of people came to the faith. Many were curious about how so many who were entrenched in a culture that venerated ancestors were able to have such a complete change of heart after hearing the gospel for the first time. This led to many people starting to study this evangelist's methods for evangelizing. After some observations, it was obvious that his methods were very thorough, elaborate, and well designed. This evangelist was not trained or an expert in missiology, and whenever people asked him where he had learned his sophisticated methods, he would respond, "I was absolutely committed and dedicated to the task of leading and bringing many to faith in God, and God gave me wisdom."

Doing our best and relying on God's grace in giving us wisdom, however, does not mean working without any tools—tiring ourselves out unnecessarily. Examining the history of physical tools reveals that many of those who invented certain tools were working very diligently in their fields and sought new ways to work smarter. They focused on their work, saw potential problems of inefficiency with their labor, and then crafted a tool that allowed them to get more done in less time and with less effort. These inventors, in other words, did not just wander about aimlessly looking for a reason to avoid doing more work. They gave their best and then created and developed the tools for others to use in working efficiently.

The Value of Wisdom

We can link this last insight to the value of wisdom. If everyone were to live for the same amount of time, the secret to serving God more faithfully during our time would be *both* to live diligently *and* to work efficiently with the right tools. For example, when I am recruiting or looking for potential coworkers, the first type of applicants whom I avoid are those who are in some way unfaithful to their calling or to the prescriptions of Scripture. The second type of person whom I try to avoid is someone who is faithful and yet lacks wisdom. Many times, this lack of wisdom takes the form of the person not knowing about critical tools to perform certain tasks efficiently. Little fruit, if any, will come from a person who, though diligent and having a good tool in his hands, lacks the sense to use it. I believe that many people are born with enough sense to use the tools that are required in their fields. This does not mean that they are intellectually brilliant; it simply means that, even if we have limited intelligence in a particular area, God will give us wisdom to complete the task before us if our hearts are devoted to and focused on completing the work.

To offer a practical example from my own life, I learned rather quickly never to regret or think twice about buying a book I needed. This is because I believe that buying a book on the basis of price is not always wise. No one can put a price on the truths that are able to be gleaned and taught to a reader through one book. Not reading a book because it is too expensive and reading a book just because it is cheap can be equally foolish. I learned that if I was focused on doing the work that God had prepared for me, I would be devoted to it, and that would mean acquiring the best tools to get the job done. This is not to dismiss frugality; I am merely illustrating that we need to put our calling first and be willing to make some sacrifices when we are focused on doing that work for God's glory.

A few years ago, I was doing personal research and study on the mortification of sin, and came across a 240-page doctoral dissertation on the topic. I considered buying it, but I hesitated because it would cost more than I expected. I reached into my pocket and fidgeted with my wallet for a few moments, and then I decided not to buy the book. But after a few days, I bought it.

Eventually, I bought *another* copy of that book because it gave me so much wisdom to apply in my spiritual life. I freely read, perused, and marked up one copy, while I carefully stored the other copy. The lessons I learned and the wisdom I gained from that book are priceless. If buying an "expensive" book and reading it will provide immense help to one's soul and inspire one to live a life that brings glory to God, then it is really cheap—because its effects far outweigh monetary cost.

The Call to a Diligent Life and Giving It Your All

Let us end this chapter by returning to Proverbs 24:30–31. The lazy and foolish man in these verses did not ruin his land and vineyard on purpose. It was a result that was brought about because of negligence and laziness. People commonly do not think of negligence as a malicious choice, but rather think of people as simply passive and unintentional victims of negligence. This is wrong, however, as the connotations of the words in this passage suggest ("sluggard," "lacking sense").

We have also seen that choice plays a central role in our negligence and laziness. If we are negligent, then that means that we consciously chose to be negligent. And the reason why we chose to be negligent is because of laziness. If we want to avoid choosing to be negligent, every organ of the body and spirit must be diligently active. Yet, because laziness is opposed to activity and effort on every front, a life of laziness ends up being a life of choosing negligence.

We must strive to be more conscious of how evil it is to not be willing to devote ourselves to the good work that God has set before us, and guard against even the tendency to view our work negatively, despising the labor for one reason or another. When we despise our work, it aids and abets laziness, allowing it to infiltrate our thoughts, which can ultimately (when we remember the three stages of laziness) lead to the marring of God's image in us.

This will require Spirit-driven focus on our part, and we must pray for such focus because diligence and focus go hand in hand. For someone who cannot focus, the call to diligence will not be faithfully answered. When we lack focus, diligence seems to be simply an addendum to the list of morally upright behaviors that a Christian should practice. In this light, diligence would be pursued not from the heart but from a mechanical sense of duty, resulting in a less sincere handling of tasks entrusted to us. When we find ourselves in this position, it is difficult for us to affectionately ask for the loving help of God. While we might be claiming to lean on him as we carry out our responsibilities, our hearts suggest otherwise, and the tension between a verbal expression of commitment and a heart that lacks such commitment will eventually lead to us leaving God and going after our own desires. In short, without focus, we might be able to begin with God, but we will not finish with him.

Let me end this chapter with a plea. Please do not think that laziness and negligence are minor matters. Laziness inflicts pain and damage on the soul and thus should clearly be marked by Christians as a dangerous sin. We must put together a counterattack and be willing to fight to the death against this. We cannot settle for living without any goals or standards; rather, we must become fiercely immersed and absorbed in our God-given duties and responsibilities, prayerfully relying on the Spirit to give us diligence and focus. This last element is critical. Wellington Boone once said, "You cannot go where you have not prayed." Truly, we will not find ourselves diligently walking the road God has set us on if we do not pray for this. Praying for such a life brings joy to God's heart, for such a life reflects the proverbial wisdom we have been studying throughout this book.

5

The Way of a
Hedge of Thorns
(Proverbs 15:19)

The Way of a Hedge of Thorns

As we have examined passages from the book of Proverbs, we have seen much about how laziness works and to what end it drives us. It should be clear by now that laziness is not an occasional enemy, we must fight against it for the rest of our lives. Yet, because of its subtlety and pervasiveness in human behavior, we do not find many people who have beat their breast and truly repented of it (see Luke 18:13). That is why laziness is far more dangerous than we tend to realize.

In this chapter, we explore Proverbs 15:19: "The way of a sluggard is like a hedge of thorns, but the path of the upright is a level highway." In this verse, we learn another characteristic of laziness through the unusual pairing of "the upright" with "a sluggard." In

Hebrew poetry, parallelism is used to either compare or contrast two phrases. Following this structure and principle, it would make sense for "a sluggard" to be contrasted with "the diligent." But that is not the case here. The reason for this is that the author is trying to posit that laziness is evil, and is using parallelism to help solidify this interpretation. Also, the idea of a "way" appears twice in this verse, but two different words are used. For the sluggard, the word that is used for "way" is *derek*, while the word used for the upright is *orach*. The former describes a piece of land that formally becomes a road, while the latter refers to a street.

In addition to these two words, another word should be given attention: "highway," translated from *selulah*, which is a gerund from the verb *salal*, meaning "to raise up." In Genesis 28:12, Jacob sees a ladder from heaven in a dream. The word that is used for "ladder" in that verse is *sulam*, which is derived from *salal*, and is very useful for understanding "highway." In some sense, the "highway" mentioned in this verse can be envisioned as a wide road that reaches all the way into heaven. In other words, the way of the sluggard is wide and, after much travel, officially becomes a road, but it eventually grows a hedge of thorns. The way of the upright is very narrow at first, but after traveling for a bit, the person who walks it finds that it turns into a wide and extended highway that reaches heaven.

Now, we must also remember that the text says "the way of a sluggard is like a hedge of thorns," so the author is not saying that the way of the sluggard *is* a hedge of thorns, but only that it is *like* a hedge of thorns. We will explore the meaning of this verse more deeply in the following pages.

The Choice of the Sluggard: Unfollowed Dreams

In this verse, we learn that the sluggard makes choices with the aim of having a pleasant and easy journey. We also come to realize how many of us think about our lives this way by default. In fact, the Hebrew word *derek* can also mean "way of life." In other words, our way of life is shaped and directed by ease and comfort. Why do we do this?

In part, as we saw early on, we may do this because we lack captivating dreams. Or, if we have dreams, we do not put in place any plan to achieve them; our dreams remain wishes. What sets apart those who have wishes from those who have real dreams is that real dreams give birth to visions, which take shape in detailed, realistic, daily goals. Visions call for sacrifice, not ease and comfort.

We live in a world that encourages us to dream, but dreaming dreams does not demand any kind of sacrifice. Dreams paint a hypothetical picture in our minds of what could be, but this does not demand blood, sweat, and tears; dreams call for creativity and longing, perhaps, but not hard labor. Labor only sets in when we put goals in place to accomplish the realization of our dreams. But when we do so, the dream has become a vision—something we are working toward with daily and sustained effort. By contrast, when we are lazy, we do not set goals, or if we do, we quit before we get very far, offering an array of excuses, some more respectable than others, but all of them hollow in one sense or another. And no matter how hard people try to persuade us to do something—even appealing to the glory of God—we spout off excuse after excuse. Oftentimes, we really have one intention: to live a life that is comfortable and requires the least amount of exertion. If living a life that brings glory to God requires more than this, then, sadly, we practically resign ourselves to live as nominal Christians rather than Christians of the cross. Christians of the cross know that theirs is a cruciform life, and that they should expect to suffer and sacrifice for God's glory, following in the footsteps of Christ himself. Remember that the glory of God led Christ to Golgotha, not to the world's greatness.

When we avoid sacrifice and churn out excuses, we epitomize those whom the Bible describes as the people whose god is their stomach (Phil 3:19). "Stomach" in the original Hebrew context referred to the intestines, which is where the seat of human desires dwelled. In one sense, the meaning of this verse (Phil 3:19) could be interpreted as follows: one's god is what one wants to do. This not only rings true to our contemporary experience, but also reflects the ancient evil of idolatry. Just as idolatry leads to ruin, so does laziness.

But notice the painful paradox of laziness, which we referenced earlier. Laziness, eventually, will not be the absence of work; it will simply be the replacement of God's work with Satan's work—evil desires of the flesh. When laziness takes root in our lives, our road seems very easy at first. We dodge responsibilities, hold off obligations, and set ourselves at ease. We pretend that we can do whatever our hearts desire—eat, drink, and be merry (Luke 12:19). But merriness turns to melancholy, and melancholy to maddening desire. Eventually, we will be faced with pain and sorrow more spiritually crippling than we could have imagined. A life of godless ease is bound to be a life of worldly disease.

Hopefully, we never get that far on the road. Hopefully, by

God's grace, we become conscious of where our road is leading and awaken our souls from slumber. The only way to walk in the other direction is to set detailed goals and begin achieving them in prayerful reliance on the Spirit. We cannot content ourselves with simply being aware of the problem of laziness. There are countless alcoholics who are aware of their alcoholism, but awareness is not a solution; it is only a beginning. Intentional steps toward recovery must be planned and executed with the help of others. So it is with our laziness. If we desire to be free of it, we must have a plan in place for our recovery—and that plan should involve prayer, Scripture, and the care and direction of brothers and sisters in the body of Christ. This plan does not have to be extravagant from the outset. It might begin with an intentional personal prayer in the morning. You might even consider keeping a prayer journal so that you can write out your prayers.

> Triune God of love and labor,
> Please help me to rise for prayer in the morning,
> To lay my heart before you at noon,
> And to settle into your Word in the evening.
> Help me to get the sleep I need rather than the sleep I want.
> When I close my eyes, let me know that I have done what
>   I could for your sake
> While they were open.
> Keep me healthy in mind and body
> So that I can do what you have called me to today.
> Show me the labor you have made for my hands;
> Let me feel your strength in me as I walk through the world.

Help me to dismiss distractions,
To deal out words of love and hope,
To act with intention and pause with purpose,
To labor with love as you labored for me
With blood and sweat and tears.
  Help me, my God, to be diligent for your sake in the name
    of Christ,
By the power of the Holy Spirit—*this* day. Amen.

And after you pray, remind yourself of this immovable truth: God is faithful to answer prayer, and change will come. When expressed in specific and personal prayer, a contrite heart and sincere faith do not pass by the ears of God unheard. Such prayers reflect our desire to change, to turn dreams to visions, to follow Christ by the Spirit—and God always hears the words of those who aim to follow his Word. General and careless prayers, however, will do us little good. Concision in prayer is by no means a sin, but prayers that are offered thoughtlessly, such as, "Lord, I want to live diligently; please help me," hardly reflect a deep desire for change.

When we set clear goals and prayerfully aim to pursue them, God's help and faithfulness will ring the bells of our souls; we will hear him. More than that—we will taste and see that the Lord is good (Ps 34:8)! We will make our way through the brush and briar of doubt and find the road of repentance and gratitude, a place of healing and growth in holiness. This is a glorious thought! But if we think that this is possible without setting clear goals, we are fooling ourselves. We will leave our good intentions and go back to a life of lethargy. Like a sow that returns to wallowing in the mire after washing herself, and a dog that returns to its vomit (2 Pet 2:22), we will revert back to the old life we had—a life of death and spiritual darkness.

Remember this: a person who only listens to words of truth and whose life has no change is just like someone who enjoys *listening* to sermons but has little impetus to *live* them out. If a believer receives grace and yet God's Word does not cause revival in his life, it will be all the worse for him. Recall Jesus's words about an unclean spirit in Matthew 12:43–45. The condition of the man who was rid of one unclean spirit ended up being worse than before, since, presumably, he did not guard his life against the return of the spiritual threat. In other words, he was not prayerfully vigilant, nor did he cling to God's truth as if it were his very life. Instead, he became callous to it, and, in the end, perhaps even became increasingly hostile to the thing he needed most: God's Word.

In summary, if we find ourselves on the slippery slope of lethargy and think "I can't do this anymore," we must make specific and intentional decisions to find solid ground. If we have repented of our laziness, we must have a clear understanding of what we are lazy about, and we must be detailed in our plan to correct and eliminate the problem. An intentional and pragmatic solution founded on Scripture and prayerful petitions is the Christian's road to a life of loving labor that reflects the God of grace.

The Consequences of a Lazy Life

Now let us return to Proverbs 15:19. The sluggard chooses the wide road because it is easier to walk on, as Christ confirms in the New

Testament (Matt 7:13). That road does not require any inner wrestling with the self, or the anguish of mortifying sin; it is, instead, a relatively comfortable journey. But during that period of ease, the sluggard is exposed to all kinds of dangers that grow silently stronger and more prevalent. As time passes, the dangers that sprout from selfishness and carnal passions turn into weeds that choke the perennials of gospel grace. These dangers manifest themselves both physically and spiritually. Physically, we may begin to treat our bodies and minds as a means for sensual fulfillment, which leads to a host of ailments: diabetes, lung damage, liver damage, mental disorders, and so on. Spiritually, our intellect, emotions, and volition become self-centered. We become more defensive and protective of our own hollow righteousness and self-fulfillment and less aware of our utter depravity and the needs of others. Our will, as well, becomes very weak, and whenever we attempt to do something, we fail to persevere until the task is complete; our lives become littered with projects that we began but never finished.

What's worse, our emotional sensitivity decays while an aggressive appetite for extreme self-satisfying sin develops. Finally, when our intellect is nearly destroyed, we throw away all logic and reasoning, and only choose what is comfortable. As laziness significantly impacts the three elements of personality—intellect, emotion, and volition—it impedes our development and corrupts our overall personality.

And of course, spiritually, as the sluggard's soul rots and decays, his relationship with God is severely damaged. The floodgates of sin are let open and there is little or no resistance by the soul. Because God never compromises his character, he will not commune with one who is living a life steeped in sin, so a sluggard's relationship with God fades into the background.

Now, once again, it is not that when we are lazy we do not bear any fruit—we do. But the exact fruit that we bear in our lives is what the passage likens to "a hedge of thorns." If we are not making any effort and live lazily, but then turn around all of a sudden, we will realize that our flesh has been destroyed and our souls are exhausted. That is why there can be no harmony between those who are lazy and those who have detailed goals and are living spiritually sincere and faithful lives. "What fellowship has light with darkness?" (2 Cor 6:14b). It follows that when we are lazy, we avoid fellowship with genuine believers in order to become more mature and disciplined. Instead, we begin to meet and have fellowship with those who are lazy as well. As the saying goes, "Birds of a feather flock together." This continues until these lazy believers begin to break away from the fellowship of genuine believers and end up living in rebellion against God.

This destruction of the flesh, personality, soul, and relationships is the result of the laziness described as "a hedge of thorns." This is surely the reaping of the evil seeds that were sown in the life of the sluggard.

The Hidden Evil of Laziness

In Proverbs 15:19, the word that is translated as "the upright" comes from the Hebrew verb *yashar*, which can mean "honest, level, and right (without error)." So instead of limiting the meaning of *yashar* to "the upright," "the righteous one" or "the honest and moral one" could also be included in our understanding of the verse. The fact that *yashar* was used by the author to contrast the sluggard with the other type of person tells us that the text is implying that there is something important for us to consider. In the shade of laziness, it is easy for lawlessness, expedience, crookedness, and other noxious things to roost. Cutting corners, which may seem to be the beginning of laziness, is actually a pattern of behavior that becomes more frequent once it is practiced for the first time.

This pattern is revelatory of something else, too: a desire to live for men rather than for God. When laziness takes root in us, it becomes easier to compare ourselves to others and strive to achieve what the world offers. With God, we do not encounter this problem because there is nothing greater we could have but God himself, and he gives this to us in grace. But when we fall into laziness, in addition to grouping ourselves with others who share the same worldly ambitions, we live comparatively. In other words, we resort to expediency because we are focused on *others* rather than on God, and so our aim becomes catching up with the rest of society without doing all the work that may be required. We live our lives as if we are lagging behind men and women who have more than we do, and we become hell-bent on overtaking them, but the real tragedy is that even if we were to overtake them, we would be dissatisfied, hollow, and horrified at who we've become. How searing are the words of Christ (Mark 8:36): What does it profit us to gain the whole world and forfeit our soul?

But cutting corners and trying to live expediently isn't the worst of it. As the power of laziness grows, it leads us to be willing even to live lawlessly—as long as that means we can be at the same level (enjoy the same lifestyle, have the same kind of job, etc.) as others. This, once again, is why it is critical to consider laziness an evil, rather than a bad habit or poor character trait.

The Person Who Walks the Narrow Road

Contrast the way of the sluggard with the path of the upright man. The word used for "path" in "the path of the upright" is *orach,* which can mean either a small road or a street. This path is different from the road of the sluggard, which leads to a hedge of thorns that stretches far and wide. This is a road that reaches all the way up to heaven; although its entrance may be small and narrow, it eventually becomes a highway.

This does not mean that the path of the upright eventually becomes a walk in the park. In all honesty, casting aside laziness and walking on the path of diligence demands a lot of continuous sacrifice and constant perseverance. This is because it is easier to be swept away by the waves of the world and go with the flow, and because we encounter many people who criticize any attempts we make to live faithfully and righteously. That is why the Bible describes the path of the upright as narrow and small, and not a wide and easy road. It is inevitable that there will be impasses and obstacles that could not have been accounted for on our narrow path. There will be much mire to sink into, stones to stumble upon, and vines to trip over. There will *always* be trials and suffering. The point is not to find the path that leads us away from suffering, but to find the path that leads us to the right destination. The road of the upright is walked upon willingly by the faithful, but not because it is luxurious. It is simply the way of truth. In this sense, perhaps the fact that this road becomes a "highway" simply means that the longer we walk it the clearer it becomes that it is *the only road worth taking.*

We know from our own observations that those who live uprightly and morally are always in a healthy state of tension, a tension that results from hard work leading not to complete rest (as we might hope) but to further calls to vigilance and spiritual trials. The upright always expend energy maintaining their physical and spiritual health, and live without their guards down when certain doors are closed, or when they are confronted with situations that can pollute their hearts. What's more, those who diligently and faithfully abide by and live according to God's Word will break a sweat doing so: "the way is *hard* that leads to life" (Matt 7:14, emphasis added). In contrast, when we are lazy, we spend the majority of our time resting, and only a little bit of time actually working. But the rest we find in lethargy is not for the betterment of our souls. It simply leads us further down a road that we know ends in ruin.

To put it another way, if the life of an individual could be portrayed as a score of music, the score of the lazy person's life would be filled with rest marks, while the score of the diligent person's life would be filled with musical notes. The life of the lazy person—even if it were full of leisure—would have no melody, while the life of the diligent person—even if it were full of difficulties—would be a beautiful symphony. Which of these lives would God find more pleasing?

The Highway of the Upright

As we have noted time and again, living uprightly and morally requires a constant, never-ending fight against the depravity inside oneself that causes laziness. This is truly not an easy task. We need constant reminders that we are prone to take the easy road. Walking along the narrow path is like living a dangerous adventure, for there is no guarantee of what the future may bring. There is, however, a guarantee of the destination, and that is most important.

To help us walk the narrow road, the Bible provides much encouragement as it promises that although the path may be narrow and difficult at first, it will eventually become a wide-open highway: a clear route to the God of grace who spent himself for us. We know that even at this moment, living diligently may appear very difficult and living lazily may seem more appealing. But as time passes, spiritual growth will manifest itself in the diligent life.

Of course, it will be very difficult to live diligently as time passes if one's motive to do so is the blessings received. Truthfully, if someone walks on the path of the upright expecting a reward, he will burn out and give up walking that road even before it gets to the part where it turns into a highway to heaven. The motive for a believer walking on the road of the upright is to bring joy to God. For those who are diligent and upright, they find joy in bringing joy to God. As they consider the passion and crucifixion of Christ, they crucify themselves and follow after God instead of chasing after a life that finds pleasure in sinful behavior. Because of this, even if they were to never go from rags to riches, their interest is in holiness and not in blessing.

Also, because we learn to love walking on the path of the upright more than simply receiving material blessing, we faithfully carry out our duties—while endlessly writhing and struggling to live a holy life. Circumstances may change, but our goal and aim do not. Eventually, we will enjoy the fruit of living a life that is with God. Notice that this is not the case for us when we are lazy. Our passions and enthusiasm can change in an instant on the basis of what we see the world chasing after.

Laziness and Spiritual Depression

An upright person also has deep affection for the Word. This is because the Word gives and teaches practical wisdom on how to live as a faithful believer. When we are lazy, we hardly ever come to a clear understanding of God's Word, because we do not study it in depth or even have the desire to do so. We find God's Word undesirable, since it would by default force us to live differently. No matter what God may tell us to do in our laziness, we will have an attitude of rebellion—a mind set against Christ. With this mind, we will live however we want, while scorning the Lord and his clear, illuminating revelation.

If we continue to live this way, God may confront us and convict us through his Word at a retreat or a meeting or a Bible study. We might even be led to tears and genuine repentance. But even if that grace is poured out upon us, it becomes momentary. Whatever conviction we may have received, it is a chance for us to repent of the life of ease and turn back to the Lord. But that conviction often languishes for a few days and then disappears; it produces no lasting change. In the end, this is not true conviction, but just a temporary disturbance on the spiritual surface.

We all know those who have been through a spiritual "high" but then end up turning back to old ways. If we are blessed at a summer retreat or through a small group or Bible study, then we must follow this blessing with a practical question: What are we going to do when the high goes away? If we do not actually come before the Lord and pray earnestly for change, as well as take part in activities that would help in correcting ourselves, the alleged blessing we received would be in vain. This is akin to someone who wakes up, but then thinks to himself, "wake me up for next year's summer retreat," and falls back to sleep. It is just like the lazy farmer we discussed a few chapters ago. Spiritually, laziness can anesthetize us so that we become stagnant.

If You Were to Ask Me Why I Exist . . .

When we choose the wide road, it is because we want the easier path, but this path inevitably leads to spiritual death. The wide road has one destination only: enslavement to carnal passions. The narrow road, in contrast, takes us farther toward our heavenly home.

Let us take a moment to consider this truth in the life of Jesus, as well as in the lives of those who met Jesus and treated him with respect. In the book of Acts, at the time of Pentecost, do we see any hints of laziness among the apostles? Can we discover any traces of sloth, indolence, or complacency due to apathy or indecision? No! Instead we find a vibrant, servant-like community of people who love God and hate the world. It was not the world in general that was hated but particular practices of those who live in it: sloth, indolence, and complacency. These are gifts given by the defeated ruler of this world. Despite the fact that we are decaying physically, we must push back against the devil and fight as if our lives depended on it—because they do, not in the sense that we earn salvation but in the sense that our actions here have effects on our soul's development. Perhaps that is why George Whitefield wrote, "I am decaying daily; but resolved in the strength of Jesus to die fighting."[1]

It is bad enough that we have lived our lives to the point of breaking God's heart, impeding his glory in the process. From now on, we must strive to live in a manner that pleases God and brings him much joy for saving us.

This reminds me of a thought I had some weeks ago. If God were to ask me, "Is there any reason why I should allow you to keep living right now?" how would I respond? Would I be able to just spout off a list of reasons justifying my existence? Or would I be struck dumb? It is a good question to ask, not to encourage us to see the merit in our own lives, but to see that we are, in fact, living for God's glory in various ways. I would also like to ask *you* this question. Do you have any reason why God should allow you to keep living right now? You may be thinking, "My children are still too young and I have to take care of them," or "I'm still single, but I want to get married," or "I need to take care of my business." But, instead of those reasons, can you think of a reason that would

---

1 George Whitefield, "Letter DCXXX," in *The Works of the Reverend George Whitefield*, vol. 2 (London: Edward and Charles Dilly, 1771), 134.

get God to say, "That is a good one! If I allow you to continue to live on this earth with that kind of reason, the world may be redeemed and transformed a lot sooner"?

We are not living in this world for our own pleasure and joy. Although we do not know how long we will live, we are to live for God's glory, for he is the one who loves us, has poured out on us all blessings, and allows us to live in his presence.

No One Can Control Time

Jesus chose to walk on the narrow road. He gave it his all in staying on that path and serving God. Although his life was only half as long as many others', Jesus was someone who cast aside laziness, and was therefore able to accomplish much more than others could have done in twice the time. Whether it was raining or a strong wind was blowing, whether people gladly listened to his teachings or reacted negatively to them, Jesus lived abiding in truth with complete faithfulness and diligence. He taught whatever he lived out, and whatever he taught he personally modeled for everyone else. His days on earth were numbered, just as ours are.

You know, time does not wait for us. The Son of God incarnate wished that another way would present itself for him to please his Father (Luke 22:42). Perhaps he wanted more time with his disciples, more time with his family, more time extending his ministry. We do not know. But what we do know is that he took the time he had and accomplished his Father's will, and he did this as a model for us. As the Son of God who was with the Father and the Spirit when time was spoken into motion, he certainly had the power to pause time. But in his humanity, he was bound by the laws of time, and he did all that he could with the hours and minutes he was given by the Father.

Just as time did not wait for Jesus in his humanity, so it does not wait for us. We cannot control time as we see fit, though sometimes our actions suggest that we think we can. And there is a dramatic difference between the time God has *for us* and the time we have given *to him*. If we reflect on our lives, we will quickly realize that we have received inestimable and overwhelming, abundant grace during countless moments. Our souls have been awakened and are deeply moved by the Lord who pursues the lost; he has spent so much time on us! We have been smitten by him with unspeakable joy in the truth of the gospel. And yet the amount of time in which we have brought joy to God is so little. But this is not a cause for depression as much as it is a call to diligence. There are still opportunities for us to live the remainder of our lives for God. It is not too late to start living diligently for his glory. Just think of how every second of every day could make God smile . . . if we would only give ourselves fully to him. At every moment of our lives, we must be willing to commit our hearts, our volition, and our character to live for God. That is the best and only way to use the remaining time that we have to bring glory to him.

Beloved brothers and sisters, there are two roads in front of us: a very narrow road that eventually turns into a highway, and a wide road that turns into a hedge of thorns. Which road will you take? Will you choose the road that begins with comfort but eventually leads to a hedge of thorns, and to God's frustration, or the road that is like a narrow path but eventually turns into a glorious highway that leads to heaven, which droves of saints have walked upon before?

Proving and Affirming Our Commitment

Instead of being easily swayed by the temptations of laziness and looking for the easy road, we must look for the rough and narrow road that Jesus walked upon. Take a moment to think about Jesus right now. Although he lived only for about thirty-three years, he accomplished things that people who lived to 300 would never accomplish. Although loneliness was his friend and exhaustion his companion, he had a dream, a dream to see the countless number of souls that God created return as God's people. In order to realize this dream, he made detailed plans and set detailed goals, took upon himself human flesh, and came into this world. He spent thirty years preparing and training, and then spent his last three years in explosive and powerful ministry.

Of course, Jesus also rested, and we must rest too. However, the way in which he rested and the way in which we take constant breaks in our laziness are very different. When we are lazy, our greatest joy, that for which we live, is rest itself. In other words, when we are lazy, the break is the end we aim for. In contrast, for Jesus, his rest was a means to an end. It served his divine goal of wanting to work and achieving his goals and accomplishing his plans for the glory of God the Father. That is how we must think of our rest, for we have the mind of Christ (1 Cor 2:16).

We were created to be humans, which means that we are mortal and have an end. We were not created to be like machines or automatons that can work forever. If a machine cannot operate at full capacity if you force it to run nonstop, how much more would a sentient being of flesh need some rest and recovery? But whereas godly rest gives us new strength and stirs our souls to have good desires, ungodly rest causes laziness; it makes our souls sick, and contents them with lesser desires.

Now, let me end this chapter by saying that this proper rest just mentioned, even though it is small, has two elements that allow it to fulfill us. The first is the proper proportion of rest compared to labor of the flesh.[2] God created the world in six days and rested on the seventh in order to show that we all need a Sabbath. The second is the proper focus of rest for the soul. When we become exhausted from laboring intensely for a long time, our focus on achieving good-intentioned spiritual goals will be lost. Although we need the physical strength to achieve good goals that we set for God's glory, our souls also need to use, maintain, and retain the passion to achieve those goals. Therefore, we cannot simply rest from physical labor and expect to be fully recharged and ready to work again. When we decide to rest from physical labor, we must allow our souls to focus and concentrate on things that are good. The flesh may be granted rest by forgoing the duty of labor, but the soul receives new strength only when it focuses on the Lord. After all, Scripture tells us, "But they who wait for the LORD shall renew their strength; they shall mount up with wings like eagles; they shall run and not be weary; they shall walk and not faint" (Isa 40:31).

---

2 The biblically suggested ratio between rest and labor is six days of work and one day of rest. That is the "golden ratio."–Trans.

Jesus, remember, also invites us to rest (Matt 11:28) and commanded his disciples to rest (Matt 26:45; Mark 6:31, 14:41). Nevertheless, this rest was not for the sake of rest itself, but because the rest would provide them with energy to carry out their duties. Therefore, the rest we receive in taking a break from physical labor or from our responsibilities is not the kind of rest that gives us license for debauchery and promiscuity. We must model and emulate Jesus—even in regard to rest.

I'll end with a story. There was an incident that occurred when I was serving before I was ordained. At a church staff meeting, it was revealed that there was a pastor who did not do pastoral visitations.[3] The senior pastor, although old, spoke up in a soft but distressed voice: "Is that really acceptable to you?" The staff meeting finally came to an end, and everybody rose to leave and attend to his or her own matters. However, the senior pastor was still sitting down by himself and did not seem to want to get up. Without disturbing him, I observed him very carefully and overheard him saying to himself, "How could he stand before the Lord living so lazily . . . with what honor or right can he come to the Lord working that slothfully . . ." He had an extremely grieved countenance and his head was turned away, but I noticed tears forming in his eye.

I believe that this is the heart of God, brothers and sisters. With what right can we come to the Lord living so lazily? The moment we cling to our laziness, all the good things in our goals, visions, and dreams will disappear. Victory over sin, a holy life, the

---

3 Pastoral visitations play a pivotal role in Korean Christianity, as they do in many Christian churches in the west. The church staff is obligated to visit every member of the congregation—at work or at home—without exception.—Trans.

life of a true believer, may be filled with dreams, goals, and visions, but they will disappear. A lazy life may seem comfortable now, and a life without goals may seem easy, but continuing on that road will eventually lead to a moment of being blocked by a hedge of thorns. In that moment, we will realize quickly that Jesus is not pleased with us. And, beating our chests, we will regret how we have lived up to that point.

Brothers and sisters, it is still not too late. Let us together start setting and making detailed goals. Let us be willing to fight laziness. Let us commit and dedicate our lives to serve God and to be diligent in all things—before the face of the one whose heart breaks over our laziness.

PART II

Saying Goodbye to Your Close Friend

6

Laziness and Sleep, Part 1

(Proverbs 19:15)

I'm Sorry for Sleeping So Much

In this chapter and the following one, we will focus on a common manifestation of laziness: excessive sleep. Sleep takes up a good part of our lives and is integral to the concept of rest, so it is important to give it a fair amount of attention in our discussion.

Let me begin with another personal anecdote. When I was a professor at a seminary, the commute was a challenge. My house was located in Incheon while the school was located in Anyang, which meant I had to travel almost 15 miles each way every day. The reason the commute was difficult was not necessarily the distance, but the number of cars that were on the road at the same time.[1] Most

---

1 Incheon is the third-most-populous city in South Korea, with almost 3 million people. During this time, the population density of Incheon was almost 7,000 people per square mile.—Trans.

mornings, it felt as if I were sitting in a parking lot. After wasting a lot of time on the roads during rush hour, I decided to start going to school at the crack of dawn, when fewer cars were on the road.

I would arrive at the school at six in the morning and walk up a hill behind the administrative building with a sitting mat in order to start my day in prayer. After praying, I would see the rush of students filling the campus as I came down from the hill with my mat and eventually I would get lost in the crowd. Making what seemed like a small change at the time—coming in to work as early as I did and starting off my day with prayer—made a huge difference in how I approached my day. It gave me more time to do what I really wanted to spend time doing—communing with God. Admittedly, I was a lot younger and healthier at the time, which made it easier to make these changes and get less sleep. I could do a lot then that would allow me to change my lifestyle and live diligently. As you grow older, it is more difficult to make some of these changes, but it's not impossible; it's just a matter of living as much as you can in a single day.

The late Reverend Yoonsun Park said, "Tomorrow is not my day. That is why I live today as if it were my last day, giving it my all, and using my time wisely." Like him, I felt convicted that I needed to get the most out of the time God has given me, and I have made many efforts to do so.

On one occasion, I made an effort to encourage my students at the end of class by talking about the spiritual giants of history, and how they would use their time carefully and intentionally. I then reminded the students that the choice not to live diligently is rooted in laziness, and I charged them to look at the life of Jesus, who exhausted all of his being during his time on earth so that he could accomplish the will of his Father. After I finished talking to them, I had the students close us in prayer, and one of the students mumbled something that has always stuck with me. As he was praying, his voice began to break, and then he said, "God, I'm sorry for sleeping so much." His repentance brought home to me what we can often forget: sleep has a purpose, but that purpose can easily get lost on us.

The Principle of Sleep

Laziness loves sleep, for in sleep we can become calloused to the preciousness of time. When we oversleep, our conscience dulls and our spirit of repentance dims. This is precisely why excessive sleep is a very serious sin that can bring great harm to our spiritual life. Throughout this book, we have seen that we must be vigilant in guarding ourselves from the threat of laziness. This chapter will show how this can mean guarding ourselves against excessive sleep.

Now, at this point you might ask yourself, "If this is the case, then how many hours should we be sleeping a day? Where is the line that distinguishes between health and laziness?" While there are many studies that suggest a golden number of hours that humans require, there is no universal consensus on a number that can be confirmed for every person. There are people who are born constitutionally weaker than others and must sleep more in order to function properly, and there are people who are very active even though they sleep less than others. Also, there are people who have abnormalities in their nervous system or physical handicaps and therefore cannot sleep, as well as people whose health has temporarily burned out and therefore need plenty of rest in order to recover. No two people are exactly the same.

But with the second group of people—those who are prevented from sleeping because of some physical reason and those who need an extended amount of rest temporarily—the problem of sleep divides into two types: sleepiness because of the accrual of fatigue and sleepiness because of inescapable energy depletion owing to a medical problem. In the former case, a person can recover easily by sleeping. In the latter case, it becomes very difficult for a person's body to recover, because sleeping may even worsen the overall condition of the body. In the latter case, sleep alone will not solve the problem; additional medical treatment is required. To fully recover, a person must seek healing by various means, such as medicine, nutritious food, and consistent exercise. It follows, therefore, that we must become wise in regard to the problem of sleepiness. When we are sleepy, we should not succumb to the feeling and sleep right away. Instead, we should discern whether the desire to sleep is a phenomenon that occurs simply because we are tired, or whether there are basic issues we must address consciously before turning to sleep as the solution.

However, one truth is clear in relation to the problem of sleep: aside from those whose special circumstances require that they get much rest and sleep, no one should ever develop the habit of sleeping too much. The foundation of the Christian's life is moderation—not to be excessive in anything, whether it be sleeping, eating, or enjoying leisure and breaks. We are not to enjoy these things in and of themselves; they are means of restoration and recovery for work that will truly bring us joy by glorifying God.

Tardaymah: Deep Sleep

In this chapter, we will examine Proverbs 19:15. In this verse, the author mentions that laziness will result in sleep. If we look at the original Hebrew of the verse, it could be translated as, "Laziness causes one to fall into a deep sleep, and the idle will starve." "Deep sleep" is translated from *tardaymah*, which is the same word that is used to describe the sleep that God put Adam under in order to create Eve from his rib. If Adam was not even able to feel his rib being taken from him during such a sleep, then *tardaymah* can be understood as a kind of sleep in which one's entire body is anesthetized.

The issue in view here is that the sleep that laziness causes is not just "normal" sleep, but *deep* sleep. In the original Hebrew, the language also tells us the way in which laziness causes this kind of sleep: falling. In other words, when laziness causes someone to *fall* into sleep, it causes that person to be tired constantly; no matter how long he sleeps, he is always tired. The range of sleep extends into opening time and closing time, as we might say in Korea.[2]

---

2 "Opening time" and "closing time" refer to the hours when someone goes in to work and comes back home. In the West, this would be the equivalent expression of "nine to five," but Korea follows more of an "eight to nine" lifestyle—no one may leave until the boss leaves.—Trans.

Regardless of time or place, as long as there is an opportunity, sleep will constantly look for it in order to trip a person up and cause him to fall into that anesthetized slumber.

In all of this, we must remember that the issue of sleep symbiotically involves the physical and spiritual aspects of the individual, just as any other issue does, for humans are body-spirit image-bearers. So when excessive sleep becomes a problem, the first thing we need to pray for is keen judgment. How much of our fatigue is an issue of the flesh, and how much of it is an issue of the spirit? Though there is certainly overlap, we tend to treat physical issues based on what we know about the performance of our bodily systems, our personal experience, or the expertise of doctors, while we treat spiritual issues with prayer, petitioning God to illumine us and lead us with the truth of his Word.

There are still some Christians, however, who believe that their problem of sleeping too much is exclusively an issue of the flesh. These people wrongly assume that there is no problem between them and God, and attribute sleepiness to fatigue and busyness. The real reason for their sleepiness, however, is that they are, without a doubt, spiritually asleep. Now, even if someone does *not* possess a deep and mature spiritual nature, his conscience will still bother him if he cannot live diligently and enjoys sleep excessively. But if he is deeply asleep spiritually, he will really go out of his way to rationalize his immoral and dissolute sleep pattern—as if he had no conscience. Whether such people receive compassion and sympathy from others I do not know, but I do know this: their souls will lose the vibrant colors that they have received from the grace of God. What I mean is, their excessive sleep will dull their potential to glorify God in a way that draws the world's attention.

Laziness and Sleep

If it is true that laziness causes someone to *fall* into a deep sleep, then it is equally true that laziness is the path to the soul's destruction, leading us into a drunken and dissolute sleep that quietly draws us to a cliff's edge. Moreover, it is because of laziness that the problem of excessive sleep spreads. This reveals that if laziness is not addressed, the fundamental issue of deep sleep cannot be addressed either.

Avoiding laziness, however, does not mean that one simply avoids deep sleep but keeps on nodding off—it must be all or nothing. It is only by fully exerting oneself every day that one is able to live with a clear and detailed goal, and quickly respond to situations and act in order to move toward that goal. When one is able to live this way, the problem of excessive sleep is eliminated. The importance of having a goal is paramount here. We can easily reduce our amount of sleep. We can wake up before dawn every day and not sleep more than five hours each night, but if we do not have a clear goal, can there really be any meaning to or reason for living so diligently? What, in short, are we working *for*?

When we have a specific goal, we will be so focused on bringing it to fruition that we will hate wasting any time whatsoever, including wasting time on sleep. Those with a fire lit in their belly are disciplined and have become aware of how much sleep they need, as opposed to how much sleep they want. When a step needs to be taken to advance toward our goal, we will not sleep until the work is finished. If something needs to be done early in the morning, we will wake up early to make sure that it is done—and this feels like an easy decision for someone with a goal. Someone who simply decides to sleep a set number of hours a night like a machine without a specific goal in mind will eventually give up because there is no ultimate purpose. Waking up early will become more of a nuisance and a frustration than an opportunity.

"I'm a High School Senior"

Whenever I am tempted to go down the road of laziness, I always persuade myself not to do so by saying in my head, "I am a high school senior."[3] A high school senior must do everything and live a life of moderation, temperance, and restraint in order to prepare for a bright future. Even if he wants to travel or go on vacation, he must tell himself, "After I get accepted into college, I'll go." If he wants to go on dates and be in a relationship, he must console himself by saying, "I'll have time for dating and relationships once

---

3 In South Korea, there is an important test named "Soonung," the Korean equivalent of the SAT/ACT. The college a student can attend is determined by the student's score on this test. During senior year, students and their parents devote literally the entire year to makeing sure that the student receives the highest possible score. this means sacrificing time, money, fun, church, friends, and entertainment, and more time spend in study halls, cram schools, and libraries.—Trans.

I get into college." In the same way a high school senior denies himself certain pleasures in order to focus primarily on studying, we too must resist certain worldly joys in order to focus primarily on the responsibilities that God has entrusted us with.

We must have that mind-set and attitude. Even though we want to rest and play, we must wait while comforting and consoling ourselves, "I'll rest and play when I'm in heaven." This eschatological tension—the "already, not yet"—is a healthy tension that we must always keep in mind as we continue living in this world. This does not mean that we do not enjoy life; it simply means we are intentional about *how* we enjoy it. We enjoy it as pilgrims on the way to their heavenly home.

Keep in mind here that we are not being forced to do everything and complete all possible tasks. Diligent work is personally contextual: we are each called to pour our heart and soul into all that God has called us, as unique individuals, to do. If we own or work at a dry cleaner's, we should strive to clean clothes more meticulously than other dry cleaners. If we own or work at a grocery store, we should strive to put out fresher products than other stores, at fairer prices. If we own a real estate business, we should strive to be friendlier, give clearer information, and have more integrity than other real estate agents. If we own a factory, we should hear from clients that our products have no defects or flaws, or that if they do, we are working diligently to solve the problem. If we are going to study, the goal should not just be to attain high scores, but even to gain the respect and awe of those who have researched and thought deeply on the topics we are studying. This is not meant to fuel the ego but to testify to the God who is working in us to do infinitely more than we can think or imagine (Eph 3:20).

A Lesson from John Wesley

A very important figure whose life has illuminated the halls of Christian history is none other than John Wesley (1703–1791). Even five days before he died, he traveled between cities twenty miles apart to evangelize. For sixty years without fail, he would wake up at four in the morning in order to pray and read Scripture. During his life, he preached more than four thousand sermons that were two to four hours long, wrote more than two hundred books, and went around the world at least ten times to evangelize, traveling mostly on horseback. He was able to do all these things, not just because God blessed him with amazing health and longevity, but also because he used his time efficiently.

Wesley was highly judicious in how he spent his time and socialized. If a person was not a Christian and showed no inclination to at least hear the gospel, he knew that he might be wasting time that he could use for something else. This is obviously controversial today, as most would not agree with this mind-set—some would even consider this legalistic. In our own time, just as in John Wesley's, people allowed, encouraged, and indulged in parties. Therefore, he felt that the best way to be efficient and wise about how he used his time was simply to avoid opportunities for encountering the temptations and ramifications of alcohol and other temporary pleasures that many indulge in during these parties. That is why he remarked, "… above all, I think, you should beware of wasting time in what is called innocent trifling. And watch against unprofitable conversation, particularly between yourselves."[4]

A Life without Waste

Now, I am by no means saying that we need to have excellent health and live life like John Wesley did. At the bare minimum, however, we must avoid wasting our lives through a pattern of dissolute sleep. As one lives lazily, time constantly slips away. God redeemed us with big plans in mind, but if we ruin our lives by being unabashedly lazy, we waste the thousands of opportunities that he has given us, and always wander off the path that he has set for our faith. How will we be able to stand before God with a clear conscience, or without any shame?

Even if we waste as little as thirty minutes a day owing to extra sleep (which is not uncommon for many of us), there is so much wasted potential. If we were instead to invest that time in sincere and earnest prayer, the transformation our lives would experience and the great things God would do as a result of the prayers would be tremendous. But the flesh refuses to be silenced even for a minute, and will strongly resist any attempt we make to act on our

---

4 John Wesley, "CCCLXI-To Miss A__," in *The Works of John Wesley*, vol. 12 (Grand Rapids: Zondervan Publishing House, 1968), 361; "Sermons XCIII: On Redeeming the Time," in *The Works of John Wesley*, vol. 7 (Grand Rapids: Zondervan Publishing House, 1958), 67-75.

convictions. When we make the attempt, we feel tremendous pain and resistance because of the flesh.

The moment we face pain and resistance is precisely when we must think about the cross. We must remind, reason with, and preach to ourselves, "Jesus lived in this world just like I do right now. It must have been difficult for him to wake up as early as he did, and he must have wanted to sleep more. But, rubbing his eyes, he was able to get up. His body must have been exhausted, but he was willing to work until late at night to heal one more soul. He was willing to go through all that daily, and, in the end, he was willing to be crucified and give up his life." *This* is our Lord; *this* is our Savior.

Certainly, Christ did many things that we cannot do, but God has not called any of us to do those things. He has made demands on our lives, but none of these demands is impossible. He only desires that we use what he gave us—knowledge, health, material blessings, and time—to serve him passionately and earnestly. The reason why it is so difficult to lay aside our pride is because laziness has hold of us and has tempted us to use the resources that God has given us for our glory and pleasure instead of for his.

Notice here that this is why laziness and sanctification can never be compatible with each other. Laziness causes us to fall into our carnal desires and to let our souls be consumed entirely by sin. It tears down and throws away the grace of God that has been established in our hearts, and plagues our hearts with rebellion and resistance. That is why we cannot live lazily, but must instead be willing to fight against our complacent hearts in order to live diligently.

Starvation of the Lazy Person

Let us get back to Proverbs now. The verse we are considering goes on to say that "the idle person will suffer hunger." The meaning of the original word for "idle" is "lacking decisiveness." Decisiveness is the mark of an attitude that is steeped in the awareness of a definite goal. When one is deeply aware of a definite goal, he is quick to respond and react to that goal and anything related to it. The lazy person, however, does not have a definite goal, and therefore he tends not to be quick. Thus, it is inevitable that he will starve. This starvation is not referring to a starvation of the flesh, but a starvation of the soul. In other words, the soul of the one who lacks goal-oriented quickness and agility will starve.

Beloved brothers and sisters, how is your soul? If you think that your soul is starving and is exhausted, a definitive goal will be formed: restoring your soul and developing a beautiful and intimate communion with God again. With that goal in mind, let us together move with quickness. If there is any brokenness in you, God's Word will mend it. If you are lacking strength, earnestly seek the grace of the Holy Spirit. Knock and Christ will open the door (Matt 7:7). If there is anything in you that is spiritually compromised or diseased, let the Spirit, through the Word, perform surgery on you. Jesus reminds us in Matthew 5:30, "And if your right hand causes you to sin, cut it off and throw it away. For it is better that you lose one of your members than that your whole body go into hell." Think of this verse in the context of spiritual surgery, and understand that the Spirit will also remove any residual pessimism about what God can and will do through you.

Then start again toward the goal, with firm faith and a steadfast heart.

Definite Goals Call for Decisiveness

There is no use in telling ourselves over and over again, "All right, I'll start doing what I need to do and living how I am supposed to live tomorrow." The person who knows what to do but has not started to live it out is precisely the one who has no decisiveness. When we are lazy, remember, we can still appear to have goals, but they are not real goals; they are only superficial and, in that sense, nonexistent.

Every believer who has been redeemed has a definite goal: to become a genuine Christian whom God is proud of, no matter what. By the grace of the Holy Spirit, who is fighting for us against our old and corrupt nature, we can attain this goal. The problem comes when we begin to lose the desire and willingness to strive toward the goal that God has given us. When that happens, our hearts begin to get hazy and we grow indifferent. But when that goal is clear and definite, we will move. No matter how weak our bodies are, no matter how little we may have, no matter how old we are, we will push on. When our goal is clear and definite, we will be able to move with decisiveness.

Think of it this way: terminally ill patients on their deathbeds who hear that there is a medicine that would cure them would get right up out of bed and run toward the medicine. Patients who are bedridden and receiving treatment intravenously would also most certainly get up and take their IVs with them if they heard there was a cure. This is what decisiveness looks like: unimpeded resolve to get to a certain place.

When we lack this decisiveness, our souls continue to starve. But the one with decisiveness will slowly, day by day, become a Christian with whom God is pleased. The effort needed for this diligent sanctification comes only through the grace of the Holy Spirit, so we need to pray.

7

Laziness and Sleep, Part 2

(Proverbs 20:13)

A Love of Sleep

In the previous chapter, we saw that excessive sleep is not simply a physical issue, but a spiritual one. When we feel tired, we must seek the Spirit's help in examining our hearts to see what the root of that feeling is. If we do not, we risk falling into a deep spiritual sleep that leads to us discarding our spiritual calling and starving our souls. In this chapter, we continue our discussion on sleep by examining another verse from Proverbs.

But before we get to that verse, we must point out something concerning the existence of laziness, if we can put it that way. Laziness does not have a tangible existence; it does not exist in the same way that water or other physical substances exist. Rather, laziness is an abstraction—an evil of the soul—that manifests itself in a person's behavioral tendencies. In other words, although laziness is an abstraction that causes problems for the soul, it also affects our daily living conditions and circumstances.

Notice, however, that laziness does not affect *all* of our daily lives. Most often, laziness is not an issue for us when we are engaged in activities or hobbies that we are passionate about; instead, it rears its head when we are carrying out our responsibilities. So it follows that being called lazy does not mean that we are lazy in all things. Yet it also follows that we cannot be overconfident and consider ourselves diligent just because we may excel in one or two areas.

Sleep, however, is a special case with regard to laziness. It would be very hard to find someone who hates sleeping, or to find someone who really enjoys sleeping only a couple of hours a day. *Everyone* loves sleep. And our sinful nature propels us all to fall into a deep spiritual sleep because of this love. So laziness seems to pervade our experience of sleep even though laziness usually attaches itself to our responsibilities. Sleep, of course, is a responsibility in certain ways, but it is most often treated as an object of desire. That is why it is so hard to find someone who is not prone to falling into deep spiritual sleep or who moderates his sleeping patterns. We all desire sleep, and laziness simply invites us to take more of it.

This is made even more difficult by the fact that sleep, for most of us, is easy, pleasurable, and brings much peace. In fact, it even seems that the time we spend sleeping is the most comfortable, precious, and valuable time we have. But Proverbs 20:13 tells us not to love sleep, lest we come into poverty. Therefore, we must start taking this more seriously.

Loving sleep, not simply desiring it, is a basic personality trait of the fallen human race. Excluding abnormal and exceptional cases of those who are not willing or able to sleep, the habit of enjoying sleep dwells inside the depravity of all humans. This habit is the same for all of us, whether it is in regard to the flesh or to the spirit.

In Proverbs 20:13, the sleep that the author is telling us to stop loving is not the healthy amount of sleep that is essential to survival. The author is instead referring to the sleep that goes beyond what is acceptable for survival and leads to dissipation or spiritual stupefaction. This dissipation increases the potential that harmful consequences will come upon us, sometimes encouraging us to behave recklessly and waste our time.

Now, ordinarily, I would say that humans are not like animals. We do not simply give in to any instinctual desire and ignore all rational thought processes. However, if we sleep whenever we want to and as long as we want to, it would be fair to say that we are *acting* like animals, since such behavior suggests an ignorance of thoughtful engagement. Think of this from the side of animals: have you ever seen a pig set an alarm clock before wallowing in the mud? Of course not, but pigs would recognize their own behavior in a human who lies down on a whim and sleeps through the heat of the day.

The Two Types of Sleep Scripture Discusses

Now, the reason why God tells us not to love sleep is that the world's understanding of sleep makes our hearts and souls dark and dull. But the Bible's understanding of sleep is quite different. When Scripture talks about sleep, it often refers to the sleep that God gives to those whom he loves. Psalm 127:2, for example, mentions that God gives sleep to those he loves, and this kind of sleep is a gift of grace in the context of communion with God. As such, the gift of sleep is given generously to provide Sabbath-like rest for our body and soul. That is why those who receive this grace are able to sleep deeply and well—and to the right end (recovering strength to glorify God).

Those who are lazy and love worldly sleep prefer this verse to many others, even more so than do those who have genuine communion with God. Those who sleep excessively and are slothful use this verse to soothe their conscience and justify their behavior. And if thinking and acting this way is wrong, then it is equally dangerous. If we or others we know find ourselves habitually falling asleep during worship and take comfort in Psalm 127:2, we must turn immediately to Acts 20:9. If all sleep is given by God because he loves us, then why did Eutychus fall asleep and plunge to his death? Notice here that rationalizing and justifying our behavior by twisting Scripture is a grave sin.

It follows from this previous point that if Scripture tells us sleep, in some instances, is a gift that God gives to those he loves, then this means that sleep is a sin in other instances. Sinful sleep appears in the flesh as well as in the spirit, but the clearest example of sinful sleep appearing in the flesh is Jonah's sleep in Jonah 1:5. Instead of going to Nineveh as God told him to, Jonah boarded a ship to Tarshish. While he was on the boat there was a severe storm that endangered all who were on board, and yet Jonah was down in the inner part of the boat, fast asleep! He did not know how to wake up from that sleep because he was enjoying a deathlike slumber that blinded his soul.

We could go on here. There are numerous examples of sinful sleep originating from a sinful heart, most notably in Isaiah 56:10. We could examine the spiritual slumber of the leaders and prophets of Israel who did nothing to warn the people, as well as the deep sleep of Israel that prevented the people from hearing God's Word. Scripture is full of warnings against sinful sleep.

Dissolute Sleep Saps the Soul of Vigor

The laziness of the flesh that manifests itself in dissolute, stupefying sleep always brings harmful results to our spiritual life, but such results may easily escape our notice because they manifest themselves in changelessness. Or they come to the surface by poisoning our attitude at the start of each day.

For example, suppose you are lying in bed. You are not sleeping late out of necessity, nor is your body in pain. You simply do not want to get up; you would rather stay buried under your sheets. Although the sun has been up for a while, you are drooling and dreaming the day away. You continue sleeping until you are exhausted, and even get headaches. Your back begins to hurt from lying down for too long, and you only get up because you have to use the bathroom. At that moment, what will your spiritual posture be like if you finally decide to sit up and then get dressed? Will you be more ready to take on the day? Probably not. Instead, you will likely feel as if the bright sun is rebuking you. Your body will not feel healthy or energetic; your mind will be blank. If you feel like this, it would not make much of a difference if you went inside a chapel or sanctuary to pray, since your soul would not have any strength or motivation. The decision to stay in bed would have colored the rest of the day for the worse, setting you up to make poorer decisions than you might have otherwise made. This is one example of how dissolute sleep negatively influences our souls by shaping our attitudes.

Now, the reason why dissolute sleep harms our souls is because it starts with laziness. Our souls, remember, are given life and hope through the gospel, but laziness clouds our awareness of this life and hope and encourages us to remain stagnant. There can be no coexistence of the gospel with laziness; we always choose to focus our attention on one *or* the other. If we try to reconcile laziness with our commitment to the gospel, we will never truly enjoy the abundant spiritual blessings that are offered to us in Christ.

By now, it should be clear that we cannot assume that sleeping is simply something that we do. There is a fine line between a proper, rejuvenating amount of sleep and an excess that tends toward evil. It follows, then, that when we become deeply aware of the dangers of a dissolute sleeping pattern, our hearts should break in front of God for all those days that we have wasted sleeping.

The numerous days that we have been given were gifted by God in order that we might serve and glorify him, not for our own amusement or selfish leisure. The latter is far more prevalent than we would like to admit. If a person sleeps an extra hour every day, that is 365 hours in a year, and 3,650 hours in ten years. So much could have been done in those 3,650 hours that have ultimately been wasted. Wasted time is nothing else if not one of the many remnants of sin in our lives. The underlying cause of our wasted time is often the ancient assumption that our life is our own. If we believe that our life is the sole possession of the self, then we will justify living any way that we want to. Like a great traitor before the true king, we attempt to seat ourselves on God's throne, which is the epitome of sin. If, however, we believe that our life belongs to God—indeed, that our life is hidden in Christ (Col 3:3)—then we will strive to live *for him*. As the Apostle Paul says in Ephesians 6:6–7, we will do "the will of God from the heart, rendering service with a good will as to the Lord and not to man."

If You Want to Escape . . .

Even though we can easily identify excessive sleep as harmful to the soul, it is not an easy problem to fix. The only hope for those who aim to rid themselves of this habit is to seek and pursue God's grace—in Christ and by the power of the Holy Spirit. Sleeping less, though it might seem insignificant, is actually a work of God in the believer's life. Praying and meditating daily on Scripture is an integral part of the solution. Though it may seem strange to think this way, sleeping *less* is a manifestation of God's grace and faithfulness to us.

But we must be careful not to underestimate our need for the continuous grace of God in this or the amount of work and time and energy that such a change will demand of us. In other words, we do not just need a small measure of grace to recover from a pattern of excessive sleep. Part of the reason for this is that our personality does not change immediately once some measure of grace is received. Reading a Bible verse that inspires and energizes us one day may seem like the holistic solution, but how will that same verse affect us the following week? Chances are, we will still lapse into our bad habits, so this is an issue of continual sanctification. We must commit ourselves over the long haul to begging, in Christ's name, for the grace to change, knowing that he is *always* faithful to provide it.

Now, I want to caution you at this point about extremism. The most common mistake that I see people make in this process of wrestling with excessive sleep is to attempt to rid themselves of any desire for and love of sleep whatsoever. They aim to get as little sleep as humanly possible, going from getting too much sleep to getting not enough. This is an attractive approach because it plays to our Spirit-induced desire to conform to Christ's image: to be holy as God is holy, having nothing in our lives that mars the glory of God. But this approach is not sustainable. It frustrates us and can end up doing more harm than good. What we need is not to replace too much sleep with no sleep at all, but to replace a love of sleep with a deeper and greater love of God. This is the path not only to recovery but to moderation, which can be extremely difficult for us to learn.

Think of it this way. The best way to take a toy away from a child is to replace it with something better. When the child is tempted with something more appealing, she is able to lay down what was very precious to her and take up what is being offered. Contrast this with the "extremist" alternative: taking a toy away from a child and leaving her with nothing will not result in change (as every parent can attest!). Instead, it results in tears, anger, and retaliation. More to the point, it reinforces for the child that she should fight with all that is in her to grip the next toy she picks up as if her life depended on it.

The solution to excessive sleep is very similar to this analogy. To the person who is on fire for God, sleep is not the issue. When he goes to sleep, he closes his eyes looking forward to waking up early in the morning and going to morning prayer to meet the Lord: the triune God is his greatest desire. It will be OK on occasion to lack sleep, but he will cry and suffer a nervous breakdown if he cannot spend much time in deep and intimate fellowship with God. That deep and unquenchable desire for God is what we must strive for and cultivate. We can always get too much sleep, but we can *never* get enough of God.

If we believe that we have received grace from God and have been called into fellowship with him as Christians, and yet we have not resolved the issue of excessive sleep in our life, we must really ask ourselves if that grace has truly transformed us in the way God desires: replacing our love for all other things with a passionate love for and devotion to God himself. Grace, we must remember, is always accompanied by sanctification. If we profess the name of Christ but make little effort to conform to his image, then we risk making a travesty of amazing grace and hurting the witness of the church, which is meant to be salt and light for a dark and decaying world.

In short, if we truly and deeply love God, we must be willing to suffer and struggle daily to become more holy and Christlike, replacing our love for excessive sleep with a love for God. Christ gave up everything, even his own life, out of love for the Father. That love is what we should be after, for everything else will pale in comparison. Sleep will seem a little thing in contrast to the growing, unending love we have for the God who gave himself for us.

Waging the Good War

So we must remember that the amount of time we spend sleeping does not decrease instantly when we receive grace, but over time must be replaced by fervent and unyielding love for the triune God. God must be the center of our universe: all our emotions, ambitions, and relationships must be set in orbit around him. He must remain the center of all that we are, and our continual, Spirit-led effort to make this happen is part of the biblical process of sanctification. When that process grows weak, it means that our love for God is also growing weak, or perhaps our reliance on something is attempting to push God out of the center. In the case of sleep, when our love for it remains, this is a false love, and it prevents us from loving God devotedly and walking in his ways.

Now, when we are at this point (and we may often find ourselves here), it is critical that we wage "the good war," that is, we wage war against the passions of the flesh, against the old self (Col 3:9–10). We must consider our old sinful self an adversary. That adversary fights at the behest of his captain (Satan himself), who aims to cripple and destroy us with his principalities and powers (Eph 6:12). Surely, for our enemy a weapon of choice is our old sinful self, who may at times suggest that we should fall into a deep and unending sleep and forget about the war we are caught up in.

Our weapon—far stronger than any adversary we can imagine—is the Word of God, the sword of the Spirit (Eph 6:17). Gripping the handle of that blade, we must be aware that we are always being tracked before we are attacked. The evil powers that are set against us are watching for moments to step in and let laziness take control. So we keep watch over our lives, over our habits, over our conversations and thoughts. We look at our eating and sleeping patterns in light of our enemy's advances (and his past victories in our lives), and note which conditions in our lives have led to our choosing sleep over love for God. We also must never forget those moments when the Spirit works in us and strengthens us so that we can avoid unnecessary sleep. Spiritual warfare, in this sense, means remembering the defeats as well as the victories in our past, gleaning wisdom from our experience in order to fight more resolutely in the present and future.

Like our old sinful self, the pattern of dissolute sleep is an enemy that we must kill. And if we do not, then he will be attempting to kill us. There is no point at which both sides rest. There can be no treaty between God and the devil, no talks of truce between light and darkness. In a similar sense, we cannot be content to compromise with laziness. When we do so, we resemble those who are living in darkness.

Let us contrast, for a moment, the life of a lazy believer with the life of the diligent believer (of course, we can think of many times when we are the former rather than the latter). While the lazy believer is sleeping away because he yielded to his carnal desires, the faithful believer is praying and fighting with himself as he cherishes God's love. While the lazy believer stays in his warm bed because of weariness and fatigue, the faithful believer takes his tired body to church and serves the Lord of glory. While the lazy believer sits in front of the TV and laughs at crude comedy, the faithful believer soaks up the Word of God while his heart is being filled with God's grace.

Now, let me ask you this: will God use both of these kinds of Christians in the same way in redemptive history? Will God choose a task that requires dedication and perseverance and hand it to the Christian who is still in bed? Of course, God *could* do this in order to call the lazy Christian to repentance, but Scripture suggests that this is not the norm. Instead, in the drama of redemptive history, the lazy person is an extra while the diligent person plays a significant part.

How Long Should I Sleep?

In answer to the question, "How long should I sleep?" we must begin by noting that the heart of someone who loves sleep begins to crack and corrode. In its place is a rotting framework that cannot hold the weight of God's grace—for God's grace is not simply a gift; it is a calling into sanctified living. As many writers in the Reformed tradition have noted, the gospel is not merely an indicative; it is also an imperative. The gospel is *both* something that is done for us and something that God's Spirit continues to do in us as we submit ourselves to his authority. Yet the imperative of the gospel, while light for the heart of the Spirit-dependent, Scripture-searching Christian (see Matt 11:30), is heavy for someone who falls into laziness or a pattern of excessive sleep. This is because the heart that is filled with Christ can do all things (Phil 4:13), but the heart that has been functionally replaced by a rotting framework (self-fulfillment, materialism, apathy) cannot support anything of lasting value.

This is not a call to give up sleep. Rather, it is a call to practice moderation—to prayerfully consider how much sleep we need in order to recover our strength and return to the good work that God has called us to do. The number of hours may vary from person to person. What should be practiced by *every* Christian is a heartfelt, candid assessment of how much sleep we need versus how much sleep we want.

Again, I freely admit that there are people—owing to certain conditions and circumstances—who must sleep more than eight hours a day. But not everyone who professes to need more than eight hours of sleep may actually need that much. Some people develop a bad habit of oversleeping and then come to expect that amount to feel "natural" and "necessary." Surely, breaking out of a pattern of excessive sleep will not feel good at first, but that does not necessarily mean that it is "unnatural" to sleep fewer hours than you have been accustomed to. This may simply be the effect of making a transition that the old, sinful self, especially, does not want us to make.

In short, the proper amount of sleep is the amount that recharges our energy so that we are able to manage and take care of everything that God sets before us each day. That is the right amount of sleep; there is no magical number of hours. Each of us must find this number for ourselves and realize that when we surpass it, we are venturing into the realm of excessive sleep and its attendant dangers.

Now, one issue that we have not yet discussed is the issue of not being able to sleep. As life happens, there are times when we simply cannot sleep. We know we have to sleep, but we are so focused on what must be done the next day, or what might happen to us the next day, that we cannot asleep. When we deal with grief and other personal hardships, we often encounter sleeplessness. No matter what we do—counting sheep, thinking peaceful thoughts, exercising regularly—our eyes stay open. When that happens, we should first try to lie still without thinking about anything, and close our eyes. Meditating on Psalm 46:10 can be quite helpful here as a prelude: "Be still, and know that I am God. I will be exalted among the nations, I will be exalted in the earth!" If we meditate on this and then try to lie still, we may feel more rested. It is said that just doing this simple act of lying still and resting will allow us to recover halfway when we are very sleepy. But if we do not even want to do that, instead of thinking and worrying, we can use that time to do something productive. Reading Scripture and praying, of course, are great options.

When Commitment to Holiness Is Trampled Upon

Our commitment to sleep just the right amount is, in one sense, a commitment to holiness. Our commitments to holiness are unavoidably shaped by the boundaries of our professional lives. Hardly anyone can set aside time to pray from two to three in the afternoon. Also, someone who works and earns a living wage cannot pray undisturbed every day from ten in the morning to noon. Commitments are hierarchical and interlocking; a commitment in one area of life influences or shapes a commitment in another area. That is why commitment to piety either presses forward or gets pushed backward—it is one direction or the other. That is simply a fact of life. But losing two hours because of excessive sleep—two hours that might easily have been spent on a commitment to holiness in some tangible way—is tragic. And yet the tragedy is common, for it is the inevitable behavior of one who lacks decisiveness in his faith.

Now, what would you do if your current job (which might begin daily at 9:00 A.M.) suddenly began requiring you to be in the office or at the job site by 6:00 A.M.? Would you be so frustrated that you would decide to quit and submit your resignation immediately? Perhaps some people would, but most people would not. Jobs are not so easy to come by. In today's society, going to work that early might not be pleasant, but if the job required it many people would do it. We have little choice, sometimes, but to fall in line with expectations—whether they change or not.

If we all had to adjust and start working at 6:00 A.M., it would be very difficult, but not impossible. Our bodies possess the ability to control our sleep, and the Holy Spirit also helps us when we prayerfully look to God and ask him to give us what he requires.

We Cannot Rest Now

People who can control their sleeping patterns do not do so because it is easy. Just like everyone else, they have the desire to enjoy the pleasures of sleep. If it was difficult and exhausting for even Jesus to be vigilant against laziness and to moderate his sleep—and he was sinless—how much more so will it be for us?

This is why Paul tells us in 2 Timothy 4:7–8, "I have fought the good fight, I have finished the race, I have kept the faith. Henceforth there is laid up for me the crown of righteousness, which the Lord, the righteous judge, will award to me on that day, and not only to me but also to all who have loved his appearing."

Even now, there are many people who get up early to go to morning prayer or go up on a mountain late at night in order to meet the Lord. They do this because they desire to be more like Christ, and follow after him. They do this because their love for God far outweighs their love of sleep.

Beloved brothers and sisters, let us be like these people and ask God to work in us. There is not that much time left in this world. Before long, we will enter into the eternal Sabbath, and when that moment comes, there will be no need for sleep. We will also not need to worry about constantly feeling exhausted and defeated by the desire for excessive sleep. In that day, we will come upon an incomparable, ineffable rest that can never be experienced in this world, and it will be sweeter than we can imagine, sweeter even than peaceful, uninterrupted sleep.

Now, however, is not that time. Now is the time for us to stay awake and be vigilant, tightening our belts and living courageously. Our eternal Sabbath will come soon enough.

8

Laziness Hates Passion
(Proverbs 19:24)

In the last two chapters, we learned how sleep can easily be misused when laziness takes hold of us. In looking at Proverbs 19:15, we learned that excessive sleep can starve our souls. Our discussion of Proverbs 20:13 revealed that excessive sleep can become an object of love, which fights for a place of prominence with our professed love for God. In trying to purge our lives of the habit of sleeping too much, we must replace a love for sleep with a greater love and passion for God. In this chapter, we will discuss how laziness is actually opposed to that passion. In fact, laziness is opposed to all types of passion, as Proverbs 19:24 makes clear.

Laziness Does Not Like Finishing Well

Proverbs 19:24 points us to a hidden characteristic and tendency of laziness. Laziness pushes us to have very weak responses to things that are good and worthy of our time and attention, but we might not realize this upon a cursory reading of the verse.

The writer of Proverbs tells us, "The sluggard buries his hand in the dish, and will not even bring it back to his mouth." The sluggard mentioned here is not someone who does absolutely nothing and stands idle. Rather, he is someone who understands that he needs to eat, and therefore puts his hand into the bowl of food before him. Up until this point, there are no problems. All of us would do the same. Of course, we would then actually eat what we have taken, and here is where the difference lies. The sluggard does not bring the food to his mouth; he never completes this basic step in the eating process!

What do we learn about laziness from this proverb? Well, many people think that being lazy is simply not doing any work or not responding whatsoever to anything. But we can see from this verse that *not finishing an action* is a characteristic of laziness. We can look at this characteristic more closely in order to gain two kinds of wisdom: (1) wisdom for daily living and (2) wisdom for spiritual living.

Prepare for More Than What You Need

Let us first consider the issue of not finishing what we start. What does this look like in our daily lives, and what biblical wisdom can we acquire to address it?

Even if we set clear and detailed goals, there are times when it becomes impossible to achieve them and when we must cut our losses and give up in the middle. Given that this happens to us even when we are dedicated to achieving a goal, we must begin working toward the goals we make with overflowing enthusiasm, actively responding to adverse circumstances in order to achieve those goals. Otherwise, if we work toward a goal with only moderate enthusiasm (or even no enthusiasm at all), we will end up tossing in the towel because it seems to demand too much of us. If we start by putting forward the bare minimum, we should not expect to arrive at the finish line. Instead, we must put in all our focus and push ourselves to the limit in order to achieve our goal. If at that point we fall short of the mark, then at least we will know it was not for lack of effort. We can then begin to examine the situation to see what God is teaching us.

Marathon runners run 26.2 miles (42.195 km). I spoke with one marathon runner who said that a runner is able to run only two-thirds of the distance (at most) in the right state of mind. The remaining one-third or more requires much more fortitude to complete, for many people suffer mental breakdowns and give in to exhaustion at this point. I really appreciate the wisdom he offers in regard to completing marathons. He said that when one competes in a marathon, it is best to not think of the actual destination as 26.2 miles away—otherwise, one will collapse from exhaustion long before reaching it. Instead, it is ideal to imagine the destination a lot farther away than 26.2 miles in order to complete the race. Then one will be more mentally prepared for the difficulty.

Most of us are not marathon runners, but we can learn something from this. Whatever work we may do, if it requires 80 percent of our energy, we should prepare to expend 100 percent. When we plan on expanding more energy, on putting in more effort than what might be required, we will have even greater chances of getting on top of our work and achieving the goal set before us. If we only prepare to expend 80 percent of our energy, we may lose momentum partway through, and then it will be a lot easier to quit in the middle. When we begin with greater momentum and with a deeper commitment, we will go further than we imagine.

There are people who think that if a task requires 80 percent of someone else's energy, they will be able to complete the task while only exerting half that amount because of their skills, abilities, and techniques. All of us may fall into this category at times. However, regardless of technique, skill, or knowledge of shortcuts, there are still tasks that require a certain amount of energy and commitment from every person. Therefore, a person who originally thought that he would be able to complete the task using only half as much energy as others may realize he is wrong and have to put in the other half of the work. This is not being lazy, for the person decides to follow through to the end and complete the task. Laziness only appears when the person exerts half the energy that is required and then gives up on the task. And the lazier we are, the more prone we are to give up.

In light of this, it can be difficult to notice when we are lazy because we seem to make more decisions than those who are truly diligent. Why is this? Well, we can make many decisions and attempt to do many things, but if we give up on all of them, we have not accomplished very much. A diligent person, on the other hand, may make only one decision to commit to a project, but then he remains committed until it is complete. We cannot assume that we are not lazy simply because we are involved in many different activities. We must consider *how we carry out those activities*. Do we work rigorously and tirelessly until the work is done to the glory of God, or do we give up at the first sign of difficulty? If our lives follow the latter pattern, then we are like the sluggard who puts his hand into the bowl but never brings it to his mouth. The only difference is that we put our hands into many bowls, but we still never follow through; we still stop short of completion, which means that our work seems to be done in vain. And, eventually, our souls will hunger for God-honoring work that is done with dedication. Just as the sluggard will become hungry because he does not actually eat, we will be starved as God's creatures because we are not actually doing our work as unto him (Col 3:23).

This does not mean that we must be perfect. Diligent workers still make mistakes, but they are usually forgiven for them by those who see their continuous efforts. Someone who is consistently late to work and early to leave, on the other hand, will not so easily be forgiven, or respected. We can try our best and come up short without losing face and while still maintaining our character and biblical witness. But when laziness works its way into our lifestyle, that trait seems to follow us wherever we go. With new tasks, our employers are quick to trust a diligent worker, but not so quick to trust a lazy one. And, if we cannot be trusted by people in the world, how can we be a light on a hill, shining for Christ, who dedicated himself completely for our sake?

If we want to be lights in the world, if we want to be God's ambassadors in the workplace, we must prepare our minds and hearts to work for ten hours a day instead of eight. That way, we will be able to complete our work with less stress and more peace, for we will not be taken aback when more than the requirement is asked of us. Going through this mental preparation enables us to communicate the gospel through our work ethic. This is no small matter; sometimes our work ethic is the only gospel someone will see in a day. If someone looks out of the darkness and depravity of disbelief, will he see a light in how we do our work? He might, if we are willing to prepare for this kind of work. If we fail to prepare our minds and hearts for this, however, there is not a good chance of our shining when light needs to be seen—for light in this world *always* needs to be seen.

No Transformation of the Soul Even While Receiving Grace through the Word?

However, the more important consideration in all of this is not our lives in the flesh, but our spiritual lives. The evil that brings us to quit a job partway through is not a small danger, for it threatens our spiritual well-being.

Once in a while, we may come across blind good fortune from the world. The supermarket may be giving away raffle tickets for special prizes and our number gets called, we may unexpectedly win the lottery, or we may find a great deal when hunting for a house or apartment. However, there is no blind grace in regard to our spiritual lives. Someone may not be doing well spiritually even though he may yearn for grace and listen carefully to God's Word. If he is lazy, it would be wrong for him to hope for spiritual treasure—to have his life's troubles resolved and his spirit lifted up in the blink of an eye.

God does not stand idly by and toss coins of grace on the dirt floor of the world, knowing that someone is bound to pick them up. He works *in* and *through* us to bring grace. When we are committed to conforming to Christ's image and pursuing God's glory in our work, we can trust that we will have God's support. He never leaves his servants to their own devices, for he cannot abandon his elect.

If you have children and one of them leaves to live on his or her own, do you simply say to yourself, "Well, he's all grown up now; he can take care of himself." If your son becomes independent at an early age, or your daughter has gone out with friends but has not come home yet, you get worried. God is similar in this regard. When we are led astray by the selfishness of our temptations and lose our faith, God does not leave us alone. He *always* pursues. His heart is for us, and he wants to show us that desire so that we turn back to him.

Yet the way in which God shows us his heart always varies. Out of the many different ways, the most common and best way, for our sake, is through his Word. In Scripture, God lays before us his great love for and faithfulness to us. As the biblical story moves from Genesis through the patriarchs and kings, the prophets and the Psalms, and climaxes in the coming of Christ, we find a God who has always acted in grace on our behalf. Learning more about this God and what he has planned for us in his Word is central to the Christian life.

And yet what does it matter if we hear the Word and are only temporarily and emotionally stirred? Many of us can likely think of a time when it seemed that we were living in faithful obedience to the Word, but then we turned around and realized that we were living as if we had never read a word of it, reverting to our old sinful ways. If there is no noticeable change in our souls—and such a change will always manifest itself in our daily lives—what is the point of studying God's Word?

Persistent Obsession with Spiritual Matters

Here we remind ourselves that a holy life does not crystalize just because we made a decision or commitment. The decision must be practically and intentionally upheld; the commitment must be practiced and protected. The kingdom of God is not a nation of people who make empty promises and commitments that bear no fruit; rather, in Christ we are meant to be a body of believers who faithfully live out our calling as evidenced in our daily lives.

Now, there is a danger here that we will become prideful or even content when thinking about our previous commitments. We easily swell with pride when we dwell on the moments and experiences when our hearts were filled with joy at the grace we received, when we were awakened from our spiritual slumber and apathy, and when we resolved to live holy lives. But that is not what God cares about or ultimately looks at. Such experiences are starting points, not finish lines. Instead, God wants us to know how our lives have been ruined by sin, and he wants to teach us that we cannot deny the disease our souls once had. We are in the hospital of Christ, nursed back to spiritual health by every blessing we have in him. As we move forward and commit our lives to God, we must never forget the depth of depravity from which we have been lifted. This is not to say that we should always be glum and gloomy, for God also cheers us on as we wage war against sin (in fact, he has gifted us with the armor to fight—Eph 6). His Holy Spirit bears us up in grace all the way to the end, so that we can boast in God alone and cry out at the end of our lives, "Victory has been given to the grace of God in me!"

This, sadly, is not the way we tend to live. Even though we may know what is good, we are weak when it comes to seeing that good work through; we either fail to commit or fail to follow through once we make an initial commitment. We are supposed to persistently resist our weakness all the way until the end, but we do not. How can this kind of lifestyle be understood and thought to have been *transformed* by the grace of God? From our perspective, we may say, "I have been awakened frequently by God and have received much grace," but from God's perspective, we are spiritually narcoleptic, continuing to fall asleep after receiving a fresh measure of his grace.

Consider how this contrasts with the life of Jesus. Remember, after all, that the image of God that lives in us is the image of Jesus, the one who sanctifies and restores us. Think about how Jesus lived his life. He lived like a flame. The wick of his life was lit in Bethlehem on a starry night, and from that moment on, he burned with Spirit-driven power to carry out the will of his Father. His life ignited faith and transformation in those around him, and it would not be put out until the cross. But even then, the light of life itself could not be extinguished. He rose from the grave and continued to burn brightly for God and even now intercedes for us! Christ is an undying flame. That is how he lived. Throughout his days on earth, he responded passionately to God's Word, and personally practiced what he taught without allowing the truth to fall to the ground in vain. He loved all—even the one disciple who would betray him—until the end, and taught the truth even though it led him to be crucified on the cross (John 13:1). This is the life that we should desire to model our lives after.

A person does not prove that he has the love of God by being deeply moved at the thought of God, but by being obsessed with the spiritual call to glorify God in every corner of his life. Jesus glorified the Father with his unparalleled love, never wavering in his commitment or giving less than all of himself for our sake. *That* is the love of God for us.

This love of Jesus transcends all things, so that neither death nor suffering can cut through it. No trial, no extent of persecution, no amount of grave danger can impede or cut us off from this indestructible love. In the end, it is this indestructible love that persuades us to beg for the Spirit's aid in equipping us daily to live for Christ.

Persevering to the End

Brothers and sisters, what would have happened to us if Jesus Christ gave up easily like we do, and, instead of going all the way, turned around in the middle or at the end of it all? We would most likely be spending our lives wandering in a rugged wilderness because we caused the Lord of glory to suffer by our own sin. It follows, then, that this idea of never giving up even though we are tired and exhausted, and persistently chasing after whatever might bring God a glimmer of glory, is not unfair. We must daily be diligent in putting on Christ (Rom 13:14), in wearing his love and living for him, so that we are bent on bringing him glory in every task we take up.

We work toward this goal not as individuals, but as the united body of Christ. Communally, do we not desire to see all believers become genuine and cause God to be filled with inexpressible joy? This passionate yearning is the community mind-set of the body of Christ. When we fall, we pick each other up. When we are too weak to walk, we crawl shoulder to shoulder, fighting the good fight until the end (2 Tim 4:7). In fighting to bring God glory through our everyday, concrete tasks, let us not yield to laziness. And, if we do, let us be quick to accept the rebukes of brothers and sisters who call us out and invite us to hold up high the grace we have been given in Christ.

Living Like a Flame

Let me end this chapter by saying that we experience too much failure simply because our souls are bored with things incomparably dim when set next to the glory we can bring our Lord and Savior. We must put down our boredom and pick up the cross, refusing to get caught up and twisted in sin—trying to live for God but then dying in the middle of our attempt.

Remember, the believer cannot be separated from the love of God in Christ. There is nothing holding us back—neither fewer joys, nor pain, nor principalities, nor angels, nor even death itself! It is through this love, and this love alone, that we receive more spiritual strength than we can imagine. As we call out for this love to empower us, God is faithful to give us his Spirit to bear us up so that we can burn with a desire to glorify God in our work.

If this is coming to you in a difficult moment, then my heart is troubled for you and with you. But please do not give up so quickly. Hang in there for a little longer. We can win. We *will* win because Christ has *already* won. Knowing this, let us pray that the Spirit would ignite our hearts so that we might see the truth of God and feed the flames as much as we are able. Let us dream the dream of holy fire.

But if we choose to live this way, we should expect indifference, rejection, and persecution from the world, for to those who do not live to glorify God we seem strange—even offensive. But let us keep our eyes fixed on Christ, for this world fiercely needs our service!

In this dark world, let us burn with faithfulness and diligence.

9

When Boredom Meets Laziness
(Proverbs 26:16)

Boredom of the Soul

As we all know from personal experience, and as we have reinforced throughout this book, it is easy for human flesh to fall into
laziness, and it is easy for the human soul to be sick and tired of the
Word of Truth, in light of its weighty demands on our lives and its
constant call for holistic repentance. Many years ago, I preached
every week on laziness for approximately three months. Despite
the discomfort people may have felt about this issue, God showed
much grace, as many people repented. Together as God's people,
we came into the presence of the Lord and repented of the pride
and ignorance we had in regard to laziness, for many of us did
not consider it a sin or even something worth addressing. However, continual focus on something does not always lead to greater

understanding and repentance; in fact, it can lead to callousness of the heart. Perhaps you have even seen this in yourself as you read through this book. If, for an extended amount of time, we direct all our attention to verses that address laziness, we might start off with a contrite heart, but soon the initial shock and disgust at our laziness fades. We grow sick of talking about laziness. Why is this? Why can't we continue to burn with passion about addressing a problem that has wreaked havoc on so many spiritual lives?

Ultimately, the answer is that our sinful nature is still pulling at us, trying to turn our backs to God's kingdom. Satan attempts to use not just our weaknesses but also our strengths against us; he is pleased to prey on our failures as much as on our successes. When we have been moved by the Spirit to notice a real problem in our lives, Satan does not stand idly by. He moves in closer and tries to use boredom to draw us away from what we have discovered. Noticing a problem is only half the battle. Working consistently to solve it is what truly draws out our energy and tests our perseverance.

Consider this issue from the same perspective as a physical problem. Many people in our day struggle with obesity, and there are many books and resources that they can consult for help. Some of us may know people who are very knowledgeable about diet and exercise regimens that will address obesity. Yet trying to implement such diets and work a routine of exercise into our lives is a different story. It is at that point that people are tested and tried daily, confronted with the intimidating prospect of having to make the same tough decisions every morning, afternoon, and night. It gets wearisome, and many people lose heart at this stage.

In the same way that it is extremely difficult to completely change our eating and exercise habits overnight, it is quite challenging to change our spiritual habits. It is easy to be convicted by the Bible's warning against laziness, but what happens when that conviction is brought to bear on a concrete decision: to take a thirty-minute nap or to continue doing yardwork; to stay on the sofa reading a novel or to get on our knees and pray for a co-worker? These kinds of situations are what make it very difficult to live diligently. While it might seem easy for the soul to acquire an inner motive to live in a new way, our souls easily get sick and tired of living like that because we still struggle in a fallen world that is governed by one who calls us back to the old way of life.

When Adam and Eve were in the garden of Eden and sin had not entered the world, there was no boredom of the soul, nor laziness of the flesh. Their hearts and souls were centered on God, and all their thoughts and actions were used to fulfill the original purpose for which they were created. Life in the garden of Eden was not boring to them; it was profoundly fulfilling. They were either resting in preparation for their duties or in the middle of performing them. Their foundation of trust in God was firm, so there was no way for the seeds of laziness to take root—either in the flesh or in the spirit. The soul fell in line with the desires of God, and the flesh fell in line with the desires of the soul.

But then sin entered, and God's perfect world was fractured. The flesh and soul exchanged their harmonious relationship for one of segregation and enmity. Although the flesh was able to do good works for God's glory, the soul hated doing so—or it wanted to do good works, but the flesh rebelled against the soul. This is why, in our own day, laziness is treason of the flesh in response to the good desires of the soul, and it is also treason of the soul in response to flesh that is capable of doing God-honoring work. In both cases, the treason of laziness makes a person stagnant and sinfully comfortable. This sinful comfort has never been fulfilling for humans who were created to be fulfilled only by honoring God in their labor, so sinful comfort inevitably leads to boredom of the soul. The soul cannot ultimately be empowered and inspired by anything other than God himself. Thus, we feel we must turn to something or someone to break the strain of boredom, and that "something" is almost always carnal desire.

Yet more needs to be said about this boredom. Boredom of the soul reveals itself when someone is bored with God and any spiritual matters connected to God. This kind of boredom is in fact weariness of the relationship between God and his creatures. How shameful it is to think that we could be bored by our relationship with the all-consuming, ever-working, glorious triune God! This phenomenon can only be the result of blindness brought about by sin. Ironically, such weariness toward God is prominent when we try to do what he has called us to, for the enthusiasm has been snatched away from us by Satan himself. Once this happens, our ability and desire to complete our duties, as well as our resistance to distraction and temptations, are broken down. This breakdown is similar to what occurs when a married couple begins to get sick of seeing and being with one another, and so they become more susceptible to falling into temptation. Weariness is often a prelude to broken relationships.

The Identity of Stubbornness

Sin not only fractures relationships, but also gives rise to unholy stubbornness in each of us. Yet, tragically, when we are at the height of stubbornness, we are woefully ignorant of our condition. Rational, reasonable, and godly people who are led by the Spirit in the Word of God have no need to be stubborn, for they flow with the current of God's will; their hearts long for what *his* heart longs for. Stubbornness is the response of a rebellious heart to what it knows should be done. In this sense, when we are ignorant of the truth, we *must* be stubborn because there is no other way to achieve what we want. We revolt against what we know cannot be challenged or changed (God's authority), and so in an important way stubbornness is illogical.

Now, let us pause here to make an important distinction. Being stubborn and clinging to convictions are two completely different things. A conviction is an assurance that arises from deep-seated belief or a closely held ideological structure. Stubbornness, on the other hand, is volition that arises from our irrational and carnal obsessions. While there is unity in the actions of one who has convictions, there is discord and contradiction in the actions of one who is stubborn. That is why it is extremely difficult to develop a good relationship with someone who is very stubborn. Such a person's volition is constantly warring with the person's heart over what must be felt, spoken, done, and so on.

Interestingly, many of us know that we are prone to be very stubborn and that it is an issue. Unfortunately, most of us do nothing to address it; we simply refer to stubbornness as some kind of character trait that we were born with—something that does not need to be addressed so much as coped with. Perhaps we know that our stubbornness is sinful, but we consider ourselves too fragile and weak to do anything about it. Or maybe we've just become apathetic. However, this is not a matter of weakness or fragility. It is not easy to break a bad habit, but it is possible to do so. If it were not, parents would never discipline their children when they are stubborn and prevent them from getting worse. The child who breaks free from stubbornness brings great joy to the heart of God. Just as it is with children, so it is with us—for we are still children, children of God.

Stubbornness as a Mark of the Sluggard

Let us get to our verse for this chapter, Proverbs 26:16: "The sluggard is wiser in his own eyes than seven men who can answer sensibly." Remember that the one who wrote much of Proverbs was King Solomon. No matter the time period or era, it was a given that a king would have wise men and advisors to give counsel and to educate him on matters related to his rule. Solomon was king of Israel at that time, and he had many Israelite wise men and advisors giving him counsel and educating him, in addition to the sages of other nations. So whenever Solomon would meet and dialogue with his advisors and wise men, he was humble enough to weigh their counsel and make a decision that accounted for their advice.

Solomon's engagement with his wise men and advisors is in stark contrast to that of a sluggard. In a sluggard's eyes, his own thoughts and opinions are more reliable than the good, logical, and sensible statements of seven men—and that number, seven, is important. In the Bible, seven is a perfect number. If the verse were to say "than one man," it would certainly be possible for one man to be wrong. But because the verse says *seven* men, it is implying that these men are right. So, even though what these seven men are saying and advising is right and prudent, the sluggard is refusing to lay down his opinion. In this, we see that one of the distinguishing marks of laziness is stubbornness.

A Stubbornness without Influence

Now, generally, a stubborn person seems very strong on the outside. But that strength is not true strength at all; it is a thin shell of rebellion meant to protect an anemic soul. In actuality, a stubborn person lacks self-control. Self-control, after all, manifests itself not just in resisting temptation and finding moderation, but in yielding to the wisdom of others. When we refuse to lay down our own opinions, we lose control even though we appear to retain it, for biblical control is not found in autonomous self-governance but in mindfully submissive governance: we are to govern ourselves only in humble submission to God's authority, and sometimes that authority is brought before us in the counsel of wiser brothers and sisters in Christ. Thus, provided their counsel is biblical, when we reject them, we are really rejecting God's authority. And the one who rejects God's authority has lost control of himself.

This is quite a strange position to take in comparison to the world's view of control. In the secular world, it seems that many people and nations try to control and conquer one another with knives, guns, and explosives, but that is not true control. True control is not established by brute force but by *influence*. No matter how many weapons a country uses, or how well it uses them, the country on the receiving end can maintain some measure of control by retaining influence.

Take Japan's ancient control over Korea, for example. There was a time when Japan controlled Korea and took away its national sovereignty, but that was not a conquering act, for the embers of Korean culture continued to glow.

Or consider another example. Alexander the Great swept across the known world and ruled over a vast empire. He gained control over so many lands, nations, and people that afterward he wept because there were no more lands and nations to conquer. However, once he died, the Macedonian Empire was divided into four separate kingdoms. After that, the beginnings of the Roman Empire arose at the frontier, an empire that would grow even further in its dominion. Rome was able to conquer Macedonia politically, but it was not able to conquer the people culturally—Hellenism continued to influence the culture pervasively many years after the defeat of the Macedonian Empire.

In this sense, the strength to control the world is not in the gun or the bomb; it is in the seed of influence. The one who is *meek* inherits the earth (Matt 5:5)—in other words, he who is small in the eyes of the world will rule it because of his godly influence—that is, because his heart falls in line with the plan of God, he becomes more powerful than the richest wicked ruler the world could produce. His heavenly influence trumps earthly aggression.

Just think of the way Jesus himself acted in Matthew's Gospel. Jesus rebuked Peter for pulling out a sword, and instead of fighting back, Jesus was dragged away by the guards without a struggle (Matt 26:52). Yet what the Romans couldn't do with all their manpower, advanced weapons, and resources—that is, control their vast empire—Jesus Christ and his church were able to do with ease because of Christ's holy and personal influence. Reports of who Jesus was and his meekness spread, and because of his influence as God's Son, who loved us so much that he went to the cross and died, countless numbers of people have turned to Jesus and have come to the foot of the cross. It is Christ's influence, not his physical or tactical might, that took the world by storm. It is his influence that ultimately still rules us now. And those who live in a way that reflects him deserve our respect and attention.

However, it is impossible for a very stubborn person to have this kind of influence and to empower others. No matter how loudly a sluggard cries, no matter how forcefully he asserts his opinion, he can never get someone to genuinely kneel in front of him. He does not have that kind of influence.

Bad Stubbornness vs. Good Stubbornness

Now, from the outset it is important to note that not all stubbornness is evil. There is a righteous stubbornness that clings to the truth of God's Word and refuses to be swayed. Being stubborn because of heartfelt commitment to the Word of God is very different from being stubborn for selfish reasons. For Christians, the former is required; the latter is rebellious.

So stubbornness itself is not necessarily evil. What makes it evil is its origin, its root. Stubbornness is not some neutral character trait that hangs in the air; it is a behavior rooted in the heart. It does not just appear randomly when we are confronted with a decision, and then disappear. Rather, it grows out of the depths of the soul, either from a commitment to the truth of God or from a deference to our sinful nature. By the time stubbornness breaks through the soil and into the light of day, it has already been long at work. The problem is not stubbornness in itself, but our indwelling sinful nature that gives stubbornness an ill color.

Now, if one of the biggest obstacles to a holy life is not merely stubbornness as a tendency or character trait but stubbornness that emerges from a fallen and corrupt nature, then when we are stubborn, we are actually defying God's will by giving in to a behavior that grows from a rebellious heart. In other words, the problem goes deeper than a sinful tendency; it is a problem with the heart, and that means it has the potential to affect and corrupt the rest of our lives.

It follows, then, that if sinful stubbornness is not overthrown by the work of the Holy Spirit, problems will surely arise in other parts of our lives, including our spiritual lives. Sin, we must remember, is not so easily contained; it bleeds from one life-context into another, so we must take it seriously. If, however, we are able to break free from the sin in our stubbornness, then we can grow in holiness and faithfulness, obeying God without grumbling or complaining (Phil 2:14–15). When we do this, we become tools for achieving God's plan, a plan not only of personal but of holistic redemption. So what can we do to separate sin from our stubbornness? Biblical Christianity has only one answer to this question: nothing. *We* cannot do anything to separate our sin from our stubbornness, but *the Spirit* can. In fact, the Spirit can and must do everything to turn our rebellious hearts into repentant ones. The key to unlocking Spirit-wrought change is prayer. How often we neglect the power of prayer! Yet did not Christ himself say, "Whatever you ask in my name, this I will do, that the Father may be glorified in the Son" (John 14:13)? To rid ourselves of wicked stubbornness (and to take up righteous stubbornness in adhering to God's Word), we *must* pray. And when we do, God will be faithful to break open our hearts and revive us as only he can.

An illustration may be helpful at this point. In Korea, there is a perennial plant known as the balloon flower, called this because of the balloon-like shape of its flower buds. The root of this flower is prized for its medicinal and culinary uses, but in order to reap the benefits of this plant, one must trim its roots to get rid of the bitter water that is inside them. After the shell of a balloon flower root is removed, the rest of the root must be soaked in cold water for a long time before it can be used for cooking. It is only through this process that the naturally bitter water inside the root is removed. If one does not remove the shell and simply soaks the intact balloon flower root in cold water for the same amount of time, the bitter water will remain. Therefore, it is crucial to remove the shell. This is done either by taking something blunt (like a baseball bat) and striking the shell a few times, or by cutting along the grain of the shell with a knife. Either way is fine, but one must remove the shell before soaking the root in cold water, or else the bitter water will remain.

Sinful stubbornness is like the bitter water of a balloon flower. Like a balloon flower root with its shell intact, ungodly stubbornness must be removed, and the Word of God is the implement that cracks the shell of the human heart, emptying it of bitterness. The mysteries of the gospel can then cut away the tenderized shell so that the person can be soaked for a long time in the waters of grace. After much time, the bitter water of ungodly stubbornness will be gone, and any tendencies to stubbornness will be only to the good kind, the sort that leads us to live a holy life.

Stubbornness: Pride That Cannot Be Shattered

As the illustration above suggests, a person's heart must be broken before it can be restored. The trouble is, the more ignorant a person is of his stubbornness, the less likely he is to be broken, and when someone is less likely to be broken, his sinful stubbornness grows stronger and stronger. Think of a frog who has lived his whole life in a well. To the frog, the sky seems small, since it is hedged around by the opening of the well. The longer the frog lives in the well, the more convinced he becomes that the sky is simply a small circle of light. In order for the frog to be awakened, he must be lifted out of the well by another. Only then will his narrow perspective be shattered by an overwhelming expanse of light. The gift of perspective can destroy narrow-mindedness. In a similar sense, Christians attain an expansive perspective of grace by God's revelation. God himself lifts us from the depths of our sinful well and shows us a world that we had not known before. But, for Christians, this requires brokenness. The pride that whispers of autonomy must be exchanged for humility that sings of Christ. The more broken we become, the more conformed we are to Christ's image, the wiser we become. Sadly, the opposite is also true: the more stubborn we become, the more foolish we become. Stubbornness, then, is the foolish pride of someone who has not been broken and who tries consciously to avoid all brokenness.

Consider an example from Martyn Lloyd-Jones. In one of his books he writes about an incident that occurred when he was younger. When he was at an old bookstore, he came across the collected writings of Jonathan Edwards by chance, and as he was reading through them, he was utterly shocked. He felt like a speck of dust compared to the spiritual and intellectual genius of Jonathan Edwards. It was also through that experience that he became interested in Puritan faith and theology, and of all well-known twentieth-century preachers, he is marked as a Christian leader with a great and extensive understanding of the gospel. This is what brokenness looked like for Lloyd-Jones.

Yet the majority of stubborn people are so closed off when it comes to intellectual and spiritual matters that they do not desire to learn more than they already know (or think they know). They are simply living within an armored fortress of stubbornness and pride. During their time inside their fortress, they grow distant from gospel-centered repentance and a God-centered life. Without God's grace in brokenness, they will die inside their fortress, never knowing what lies beyond its walls.

Note that this does not mean we should recklessly absorb any and all knowledge, as if knowledge is the answer to our sin; that is just another form of pride and stubbornness—a refusal to be broken by the gospel of grace. In fact, it is dangerous to read any book carelessly. Those who diligently digest the holy knowledge of Scripture and live a sanctified life develop the ability to properly discern what is acceptable as they consume and are strengthened by God's Word. Looking for knowledge without reference to God's revelation does not lead to clarity or awakening. We cannot break out of stubbornness by reading; we can only be broken out of it by God himself. Any other solution to our stubbornness will only cause confusion and frustration.

Yet this gracious work of God does not mean that we do not need to exert any energy in the process. Quite the contrary—it is critical that we make an effort to properly learn and understand the deep truths of the gospel if we want to be able to discern whether something is holy and right. We must ever guard against accepting as essential any statements from sources not founded upon the definite truth of the gospel. On a daily basis, we need to remind ourselves that no matter how familiar we claim to be with Scripture, we humbly admit that there are many components to and much truth within the gospel. We cannot plumb the depths of God's grace as revealed in his Word. We cannot have exhaustive knowledge of Scripture, but we *can* have true knowledge of it. We must cling unreservedly to the creaturely truths that God has given us insight to understand, and use these truths to sift through the sand of human thought.

Deep Wisdom Leads to Deep Humility

This brings up an important issue: the relationship between wisdom and humility. If someone's breadth of knowledge is narrow, he will be less likely to have his heart broken before God, since he will assume that the little he knows *must* be true. Rather than challenging himself by testing the validity of what he holds to be inerrant, he stays the same, and therefore risks becoming more prideful and stubborn. That is why I constantly encourage younger people to travel a lot and learn much about the world by visiting many places. As we live with and share in the culture, history, and relationships of other countries, we become a lot more open-minded and less prideful. We become humble about what we know, and, in that humility, wisdom grows.

In other words, as we learn more, we should become humbler, not more prideful. Those who have truly devoted themselves to learning and studying do not have the luxury of pride. This is because they come to realize how small the human intellect is. They realize that they only have the capacity to hold enough water for a small bowl, when an entire ocean stands before them—an incalculable amount of wisdom brought through people spanning the centuries who have dedicated themselves to the advancement of the human intellect. In this context, a good scholar is a humble scholar.

I am someone who has received the call to preach and teach God's Word. But, nonetheless, the prayer that breaks my heart the most is when I ask for a remedy for my ignorance of the truth. It is ironic that someone who studies, preaches, and teaches the Word of God knows so little in regard to truth and knowledge. I feel broken and repentant before the Lord and continually ask him for greater insight into the truth of his Word.

While this is an important element of my own spiritual life, I have no doubt that many of you deal with similar sentiments. On the surface, we feel that we are enlightened and fairly keen when it comes to our understanding of the truth. But the "gospel truth" is that, although as Christians we have been illuminated with the light of the truth, our residual noetic darkness remains. This darkness actually pitches a tent and camps out in our laziness. Laziness, remember, does not love wisdom; it thrives on mental and spiritual stagnation. That is why Proverbs 26:16 mentions that this kind of ignorance and stubbornness is found in the sluggard. A sluggard avoids intellectual and spiritual growth at all costs, so he disregards the correct opinions of seven people, and instead considers himself significantly wiser. But, in reality, he is someone with endless ignorance who does not know who he really is. A truly wise person knows his smallness and takes counsel from others, and in doing so he is faithful to his God-given, creaturely identity as an image-bearer.

Note here that the most frequently occurring word in Scripture that seems to pair well and naturally with *wisdom* is *fidelity*. Also, the pair that contrasts the most with these two words is *laziness* and *evil*. Wisdom is cultivated in and given to the one who lives diligently—the one whose passion and devotion lead him to search for new ways to be more effective at doing what God has called him to do. It is this person who understands and lives under the mystery of God's grace in the gospel.

Now, if you are not sure whether you are ignorant of the mystery of the gospel or the world of God's grace, examine yourself and determine whether you have wrestled through serious and diligent pursuit of the truth because you wanted to live a life of grace. Has your life been guided by a desire to know the true and triune God and to live in a way that reflects the glorious and radical grace of the gospel? If so, continue in this pursuit of the truth and grace, and you will become a native (rather than a foreigner) in the realm of God's grace. If not, what are you pursuing?

It is important to ask the previous question, even if you have grown up in the church. The fact that someone receives salvation does not mean he will automatically and consistently live a holy life; living such a life requires daily vigilance, regular time in God's Word, and continual communion with him in prayer. When we cultivate these things in our lives, we will be more than willing to war internally against the depraved nature still in us. Externally, we will be successful in resisting temptations and persevering through trials so that we can live out a life that glorifies God. As we try to live this life, remaining humble before the mystery of the gospel will provide crucial help and support. To put it simply, knowing the redemptive secrets that have been clearly revealed in the gospel will make us into holy people, and in this newfound, grace-given holiness we will thrive.

But we cannot use the verb "thrive" when we are still caught up in the web of laziness. This is true even if a lazy person is "well versed" in the contents and verses of the Bible. Laziness wants us to remain alive, but it does not want us to thrive. Thriving, it tells us, will require pain and sacrifice, and it is not worth the labor. A diligent, gospel-driven life is like a great pearl.

Did you know that a clam goes through immense pain when a foreign object or bacteria invade and get stuck between the clam's shell and its soft tissue? This sounds like a negative thing, but it is ultimately through that invasion and the initial pain caused by the intruder that a pearl begins to form. Likewise, the holy personality and the value of life that can be acquired through the secrets of the gospel are excellent things and incomparable to the pain endured by tearing away from the temptations of laziness and living fiercely for the Lord.

The Greatest Treasure to the Lord

Laziness causes us to become foolish. Ignorance and pride darken our vision, but diligence causes us to become wise and humble. Therefore, we must fight against the flesh that makes us into sluggards. Along with waging war against any weariness of the soul, we must fight the laziness of our flesh. Until the day we are finally called home to meet with the Lord, we ourselves must make a strong effort to not be people who have fallen into laziness and in whom evil stubbornness remains.

If we have to sweat on our journey, will not Jesus tell us, "You really did a great job! I saw how you lived your life," as he wipes off the sweat from our foreheads? If there are tears shed in our attempt to live a holy life for Jesus, will he not wipe away all tears in the end (Rev 21:4)?

In closing this chapter, let me leave you with this: there is no greater and more precious treasure to Jesus than when we diligently live and pursue his Father's will and follow in Jesus's footsteps. Making a continual effort to do this, in prayerful reliance on the Spirit and God's Word, is how we throw away our irreverent and evil stubbornness and are able to live wisely, humbly, and graciously before God.

10

The Sluggard Gives God Grief

(Proverbs 10:26)

I Cried Because of a Prayer

About twenty years ago, I read an article in a Christian magazine that led me to cry. The article featured the life of a person who became a great evangelizer after having met God subsequently to leading a labor movement. In the course of the interview, the man said something that struck my heart as if a nail were being driven into it. He had been in prison for leading a labor strike, but through that experience received Jesus into his life and became a faithful and passionate believer. Every day he would preach the gospel and proclaim Jesus in the subway. As the interview was coming to an end, the reporter asked a question and the man responded with a prayer similar to the one below.

God, I have not learned much, nor am I very prepared, so I cannot do as many great things for you as I would like. Therefore, I do not even dare to pray that you use me greatly. However, God, if there is someone who causes much grief to your soul because you have given him a great calling but he has not fully lived up to that calling and its responsibilities because of his laziness, please send me and use me instead of him! I don't know if I will do well, but I will give it my all!

As I was reading that prayer, I felt how poor our lives are when we lack duty or responsibility, how spiritually impoverished our souls can be when we leave gratitude by the wayside and function mechanically as if we deserved all the good things that God gives to us.

Know this: it is only because God did not immediately answer this man's prayer that people like you and me are able to be where we are. If God had answered that prayer immediately, we might be somewhere else, guided by the sinful behavior that blinds us to God's grace.

A Lazy Laziness

In the previous chapter, we saw how laziness leads to sinful stubbornness that shuns wisdom. In this chapter, we learn that laziness not only leads us into foolishness, it also grieves the heart of God, who has sent us to proclaim the life-changing truth of the gospel to every corner of the earth.

In Proverbs 10:26, the sluggard is described using a vivid

illustration: "Like vinegar to the teeth and smoke to the eyes, so is the sluggard to those who send him." This is not an image of a particular person, of course. The author does not say that the sluggard "is like *someone* who . . ." Instead, he depicts the sluggard with impersonal imagery that plays to the senses: vinegar and smoke, both of which induce repulsion.

A sluggard can work, you see. He is not necessarily utterly useless, but he does his work very lazily. He never really puts any effort into his duties and responsibilities, and cannot be depended upon to complete them. As a result, this person brings pain and discomfort to his employer, to the one who "sent him." The "sender" here feels pained and repulsed by the sluggard, as if vinegar were to erode the enamel on his teeth and cause acute pain from sensitivity, or as if smoke were to burn in his eyes and blur his vision with tears. The sluggard's work erodes the trust and patience of his sender, as the acid in vinegar erodes the enamel on our teeth. In a similar way, his laziness stings the eyes of the one who sent him, bringing grief instead of gratitude. These two illustrations do not reflect the deadly nature of laziness that we have seen in previous chapters, but they evoke disconcerting and repulsive feelings. In the same manner, the sluggard is a nuisance rather than an aid to the one who sends him.

The author's illustration here shows that laziness is not present only when we try to avoid doing work. It is also at work in us when we say that we will work with great diligence or passion and yet put forth little or no effort. After all, there are not many instances in which someone will boldly refuse to work. It is more common and frequent for someone to profess great concern and care for completing a given task and then not put in the effort to match his words.

There are some people who consider working in one place or having one job very noteworthy and something to boast about. That is why, once in a while, we meet people who mention that they have served in Sunday school as a teacher for ten years straight, or as the organist or pianist, never missing a Sunday morning or evening service. There is definitely nothing wrong with having served in the same position and role for a long time—in fact, serving in this way means that we can better do the task that God has given us. But there is something of more value than the length of time for which we serve. It is not so much a question of time as a question of quality: *How* do we complete our work? How much effort and energy do we put into the service?

When God gives us a responsibility or a role to fulfill, he does not do so hoping only that we will serve in that capacity or perform that role for a long time. He also expects us to be committed and make sure that good fruit is produced by our service. So, no matter how long we have spent in one job, department, or company, if we are knowingly slacking off and slowing down productivity as an act of protest or as a result of apathy, we are shaming the God of glory by offering an embarrassing witness to the God of labor and love.

Certainly, we learn this principle in the workplace as well. What is important to our employer is not necessarily how long we remain with the company or hold a certain position, but how hard we exert ourselves in performing our duties and fulfilling our responsibilities. And employers can easily tell the difference between someone who is simply going with the flow, dragging out simple tasks, and someone who is truly dedicated and passionate, going the extra mile even when no one is looking. The former works mechanically, not with his soul, while the latter pours himself into his work and, as a result, develops and grows in and through that work. It follows, then, that in order to live holy lives that honor God, we must become passionate and dedicated people in our work.

The Heart of a Manager

Take a moment to consider the perspective of managers. The greatest asset for businesspeople and corporations is not land or money, but people. When a Christian starts a business, the most important factor in the success of that venture is the faith of the entrepreneur. The next most important factor is just as important and is connected with the first: the relationship dynamic between him- or herself and the workers. That is why the entrepreneur must value relationships with people and must cherish people as the most valuable asset. When the entrepreneur does that, management is actually centered on people, and those who work under this manager will realize how worthwhile it is to be where they are. The entrepreneur can then expect that these workers will, at last, be committed and dedicated to their work and to the company.

This is, in fact, a pastoral mind-set rather than a strict business model. And, in this sense, it is crucial for the progress of our nation that business and government leaders have this pastoral mind-set. The alternatives, after all, are less than appetizing. The structure of political authority often incorporates corrupt practices, and perhaps that is one of the reasons why, every time there is a change in leadership, the incumbent curses and mocks his predecessor and promises to do better. But as he leaves and his successor is inaugurated, the cycle is repeated. Martin Luther, the great Reformer, came to this realization during his life and fought for reform.

In tandem with this is the sad truth that an excessive focus on money also leads to corruption—specifically by encouraging people to live their lives like vapor, having no eternal principle or hope that lasts. Because of this love of money, people do what they desire even though they know it is wrong, or people throw away the proper methods of management for easier methods because the proper (biblically prescribed or informed) way is more difficult.

The message I hope to convey here is not in regard to the morals and ethics of managers, but in regard to what kind of person we have in mind when considering whom we will hire. If you were in the position of a hiring manager, what kind of person would you hire? If a person is smart and talented, faithful, able to adjust to any situation, sophisticated, and has a genuine faith, no more is needed. But it is not easy to find someone that qualified, and even if such a person were to be found, it would be very difficult for any company to compensate him or her fairly and competitively. In part, this is why, when we cannot find anyone who fits our ideal expectations and qualifications, we compromise by hiring someone with the values that are most important to us. Yet, in compromising on our criteria, we must make sure that a specific value is never discarded: diligence. Laziness should always remain on our list of unacceptable character traits.

At this point in the book, it should be clear why. A lazy person quickly becomes a breeding ground for evil in any business. Proverbs talks about how the lazy person is not faithful (Prov 15:19) and is prone to corruption. Moreover, there is always a high risk that important information will be leaked by a lazy person, for such people enjoy gossip (Prov 20:19).

Yet, among the reasons one may have for avoiding the company of a lazy person, the most important reason is that such people never put in effort; they make little or no attempt to actually get work done well, and that is the whole point of hiring someone! And, beyond that, in addition to doing no work, a lazy person will actually diminish the quality and quantity of the work his coworkers produce, hurting them in the process. When a lazy worker navigates successfully through the interview process and begins working for a particular company, he will not only hurt the quality of the work of those working alongside him, he will also bring his coworkers grief, for, in moments of weakness, they will suffer by emulating the destructive habits that he brings into the workplace.

Like Vinegar to the Teeth, Smoke to the Eyes

This brings us back to the striking illustration that the writer of Proverbs uses. The lazy person is like vinegar to the teeth and smoke to the eyes to the one who sends him.

Consider another illustration from my country. There is a kind of apple, *kookkwang* (national glory), that is no longer cultivated.[1]

---

1 There seems to have been a "revival" of the *kookkwang* variety of apple. In 2010 in the city of Daegu, many markets and stalls were actually stocking and selling *kookkwang* apples.—Trans.

What made it stand out was its acidic taste. It was so acidic that when people bit into one and the juices touched their taste buds, they would shiver. That sensation, as it turns out, was quite a joy for many because it lasted only for a moment. However, to taste that sourness constantly for an extended period of time would be agony. That kind of agonizing but prolonged pain and irritation is related to the illustration from Proverbs. Those who send a lazy person out to do something will quickly find themselves irritated and pained by their decision.

What is quite sad and embarrassing is that this happens in the church as well as in the world. A missionary in Southeast Asia told me of an incident that occurred a few years ago. A church did not have a bathroom, and so the leaders decided to build a very simple and conventional bathroom. Normally, this kind of job would take no more than two days with two people. However, completing this particular bathroom took more than a week with *four* people. The slow progress was a waste of time, but what was worse was actually watching these workers work. Their conduct and work ethic was so frustrating that those who observed them were forced to leave their presence because their blood boiled in anger.

Someone once shared with me a similar story about another incident that occurred in the same part of the world. A business owner employed a young local boy who was very competent and dedicated. As a reward, the owner gave the boy an extra month's salary as a bonus. The next day, the boy did not show up—nor the next. After one week, the boy finally showed up as if nothing had happened. The owner confronted the boy about why he had not shown up for a week, and the boy nonchalantly responded that it was because he had been so busy spending the money that he had never expected to get!

Such behavior brings great anxiety to those who depend on others to complete tasks or fulfill responsibilities. In this light, firing someone unjustly is a great disservice to society, for it not only condones or accepts laziness from other employees, it also punishes those who are trying to labor diligently, and then what reason will they have to do so in the future? Instead, it is only those who cannot positively contribute to a company who should clear out their desks and leave.

Moreover, Christians must be the sort of people who are necessary to an enterprise, who play crucial roles in companies and businesses. When those who are overseeing a Christian have nothing but contempt for him—vinegar in the teeth and smoke in the eyes—owing to his laziness, then that so-called Christian is tarnishing the name of God.

Passion: The Flower of Diligence

The mere fact that we have a missional mind-set at work and then attend church on Sundays does not confirm that we are Christians. Instead, we need to live so as to reflect not just our identity as Christians but also our identity as children of God. To do this, we must have passion, but we lack passion if we do not have diligence.

We may overlook the relationship between passion and diligence at first, thinking that passion is simply excitement or enthusiasm. But enthusiasm that never moves beyond itself is not passion. Passion is bound up with action. Someone does not necessarily have to succeed in his efforts to have passion. Passion is not synonymous with success, but neither is it synonymous with excitement. Passion is action fueled by a deep-seated desire for something. So it is only when someone is diligent that passion is present. There is a complementary relationship between these two concepts. Without diligence, passion evaporates; without passion, diligence wanes.

A story may help to explain this. There was a shoe company that was deciding whether to open stores in Africa. After much talk, the company decided to send two separate people to survey the demographic and get a feel for marketability in the region to see whether the business would succeed there. After spending some time on this project, the two workers came back and presented their thoughts. Surprisingly, the reports they submitted were completely different. The first report stated that no one in Africa wears shoes, so even if the company were to open stores and make shoes, no one would buy them. The second report stated that no one in Africa wears shoes—therefore, the possibilities are endless.

In one sense, the difference between these two reports and people is a matter of passion. The second person chased after and interacted with people one at a time, and observed that these people's feet must have hurt so much because they had no shoes. He had an overwhelming desire to alleviate their pain by making shoes for them, so his report manifested his passion to help them. The first person did not even bother to show concern for the people, not even as a potential source of income. He made a superficial observation and had no diligence or passion to look into the issue more deeply.

Consider a biblical example. Look at the grit of Joshua and Caleb as they measured themselves against the burly and intimidating Canaanites: they exclaimed, "they are bread for us. God will move powerfully here today. Their protection is removed from them, and the Lord is with us; do not fear them" (Num 14:9). But the other spies did not share the same trust in God: "And there we saw the Nephilim...and we seemed to ourselves like grasshoppers, and so we seemed to them" (Num 13:33). Why such different responses to the same enemy? Joshua and Caleb had a fighting passion for and faith in God, while the other spies had neither faith nor passion. Instead, they let doubt lead them to desire no action.

From both of these examples, we can deduce that passion never forms in the life of a lazy person. Excitement? Yes. Infatuation? Certainly. Lust? Probably—but not passion. This is because working with a passion directly conflicts with the self-love of the lazy person.

The God Who Waits in Love

When we lack passion, we are more likely to become the sort of people that the writer of Proverbs is describing, and this grieves God. Look at it from a human perspective. Imagine someone who is so lazy that he makes you cringe and grimace. The more you think about him, the more irritated you become. In essence, whenever this person comes to mind, it is as if you can taste vinegar in your mouth. You grit your teeth as the acid breaks down their enamel and exposes your nerves. Or perhaps you feel so agitated, so repulsed, that the very thought of this person is like smoke blasting your eyes, causing them to well up with tears. How would you feel if someone like that were working under you, or applied to work under you? Would you be able to give him a good salary, take a personal liking to him, and entrust him with important responsibilities and tasks? If your answer is no, then your response would be similar to God's.

Yet God is not like an employer with an inferiority complex or a petty, egotistical temperament. As a matter of fact, he lavishes his mercy and favor upon us, *even while* we do not diligently and faithfully serve him. Because he loves us, he is willing to wait for us to diligently and faithfully serve him. God *waits*.

This waiting, however, is not simply waiting; it is sacrificial. It costs something on God's part, namely pain. It pains God's heart when we walk away from our faith after he has given us the calling of being his beloved children. There is nothing more that we could want, and God knows this! That is why God is willing to give people second chances. He knows that genuine believers will truly repent after realizing the grief they have caused God with their lackadaisical service, and bring him great joy by returning to their first love.

Pushing Through Even Though There Is No Passion

Now, I am not being an idealist. Although I know very well that I must always be passionate whenever doing God's work, there are times when I lose my passion or desire to do a certain kind of work. But I am always reminding myself that, even if I lose my passion, I must continue and not give up in the middle. I can find many reasons for not giving up in the middle, such as the potential regret I would feel, or the fact that I want to push myself harder to make up for lost time, or the fear that my faith will crash if I give up. Some people may even continue God's work in order to keep an important title (elder or deaconess or reverend) for their own self interest.

Regardless of the situation one may have been left with, it is not acceptable to just wait it out, giving up in the middle and hoping that someone else will come along and finish the work for us. Doing this is what causes God so much pain. Whatever vocational or ministerial call God may have given us, living it out enthusiastically is critical. We should consider the gravity of our call from God, whatever it is, and restructure and reorganize our priorities and lives in order to be faithful to that call. If we do not have time, we must give up certain roles and jobs. If we live too far away, we must move closer. If we do not have the money, we must do all we can to scrape some together. The point is a very simple one: change so that you can serve; adapt and adjust so that you can live out God's call on your life.

Before we do anything, we need to find tasks and roles about which we can ask ourselves, "How and what would Jesus have done if he were in my shoes?" Then, as we perform the work God has for us, we must always examine what our motives are, and whether we are occupying certain positions and doing our tasks with the proper motives. We must live with the same attitude and walk the same path that Jesus would walk if he were in our shoes.

Nominal vs. Dedicated Slaves

If we are putting in the effort without any faithfulness or diligence, it is because we have forgotten our place. No other creature on earth has to continually ask itself *who* or *what* it is, but this seems to be necessary for sinful humans. We are God's slaves. Although in identity we may be sons and daughters, in service we are obedient, working slaves. Even Jesus, the Son of God, did not take advantage of his identity as Son, but lived as a slave. We are, in Paul's words, slaves of righteousness (Rom 6:18), and God is the one who is wholly righteous (Ps 7:11, 116:5; Isa 45:21; Dan 9:14).

Jesus himself did not do anything for the sake of drawing attention. On the contrary, he did things that were difficult and painful, and he often did such things in remote areas where fewer people could see him. He received far more criticism and scorn than praise and respect. When we consider what he did in light of his circumstances, we quickly learn that his actions were not lofty and noble. He taught the way to life to tax collectors and prostitutes, and regularly sought out the poor and sick. Why did he do this? He tells us himself: "For even the Son of Man came not to be served but to serve, and to give his life as a ransom for many" (Mark 10:45). This is exactly the attitude and mind-set that Jesus needed in order to faithfully carry out the mission entrusted to him when he came to this earth. Jesus taught us how to serve with his life. He spent his time, his energy, his blood in service.

Leaders who have never had the company of faithful assistants can never imagine or know how much of a blessing it is. The senior pastor whom I served under before I was ordained would talk frequently about one of his assistant pastors with whom he had served for a long time. He always mentioned how this assistant pastor was faithful and diligent during the most difficult times, and any time this assistant pastor came up in the mind of the senior pastor, the senior pastor exclaimed how he could never forget and will always be grateful for that kind of service. The heart that the assistant pastor poured out for his senior pastor is the same heart that we should have, for we are all in one way or another dedicated to God's service.

Sometimes it feels as if such people are hard to come by today, and this is reflected even in the kinds of prayers we pray. There are many who ask God for something to do, and there are many who work hard at what they enjoy doing. But there are not many people who are willing to serve God like dedicated slaves. Many people may like the title "servant of God," but not many are willing to live up to it. To do that, we must learn to love humility, and that is not a character trait that most people seek out.

I mean to point out here that it is not enough to simply claim servanthood. Our service includes not just our actions but our motive. The motive for our service is not merely our identity as slaves (i.e., we serve because we have to) but our joy and pleasure in being reduced to nothing before the Lord of glory (1 Cor 2:8), who himself was brought to nothing before sinful men. Do we *love* that kind of service? Do we long to reduce ourselves to nothing so that we might glorify the resurrected Christ? If we have any other motive for service, we are in danger of being two-faced, for those who seem to enjoy service may be happy when someone tells them that they are like a "servant of God," but become very unpleasant as soon as they are treated like a servant. If we love power and are sinfully stubborn, our consciences will reveal that we cannot live this way and also take up a servant's mentality; we cannot be both servants of the crucified Christ and patrons of the prince of this world. The prince of this world is egotistical and encourages us to be the same, but one who follows the crucified Christ is always ready to step out of the spotlight and let God shine in his place.

Diligence Is the Most Important Thing

Maybe there are times when your minds are so vexed that you cannot sleep. You may be thinking to yourselves, "Why can I only do so much? Why am I such a failure? I am responsible for so many people, yet I lack the wisdom to lead properly. Can I really do this?"

There are times when I have this sense of disappointment and helplessness as well. I do not have an extraordinary charisma that captivates people, or a noble and lofty personality. The knowledge that I have attained is minuscule compared to that of others who have come before me and who serve in my time. So, when I see people being convicted and transformed through the preaching of someone like me, I really think that it is a miracle. That is why I know that I must make the effort to live more wisely, even though it will not happen overnight. If God can work miracles through me in the lives of his people, I want to be aware of every opportunity I might have to share the gospel. That is why I pray earnestly to come to the same conclusion each time I wrestle with whether I should make the effort. I continue to plead with God to help me to serve diligently and utterly depend on him so that I may not be lazy.

Again, please do not hear this as a call to perfectionism. We cannot be experts at everything or do everything perfectly. God does not desire that we do everything perfectly, either—only that we not be lazy. If we know that we cannot do something no matter what, that does not ruin us spiritually. The issue is when we *can* do something but choose not to do it. To not do something when we can do it destroys our hearts, and our souls decay because they are filled with carnal passions, for something must fill the void in our lives: either purposeful and diligent action for God or worldly passions of the current culture. Therefore, it is crucial that we hang on to this one thought no matter how difficult things may be: *Although we may fail because we are deficient, we will not ultimately fail if we refuse to be lazy.* If we can commit ourselves to this much, then we will not grieve the heart of God, and we will develop into spiritually mature servants.

We cannot give in to the temptation to do the opposite: to wait around for a diligent life to "appear" when we are spiritually mature. Maturity is the fruit of action—both failures and successes—not the result of a spontaneous gift. So we cannot think to ourselves, "I will work on being diligent when I am holy enough. Right now, I just need to learn more about God." If we are lazy, we cannot become more holy in the first place. When our thoughts are lazy, our actions are careless and misguided, and holiness is nothing if not careful and biblically guided action.

If we want to live holy lives, we must go all in—nothing can be left unmoved. Our eating and drinking habits, our sleep, even our leisure time must be given to holiness. And, what's more, we must earnestly pray that the Spirit will fill us so that we do these things with passion, not out of compulsion. When we do this, Christ will be seen in us by others, as he should be. If no one is able to tell the difference between our lifestyles before and after our salvation in Christ, then we know we are not diligently pursuing godliness.

The Secret to Union with Christ

When we do our best to live out the lives given to us by modeling ourselves after Christ, we learn the secret to union with him: his life must become our life, and his will our will. In the words of Benjamin Schmolck,

> Since Thou on earth hast wept, and sorrowed oft' alone
> If I must weep with Thee, My Lord, Thy will be done. [2]

When my body gets tired from excessive ministry and service, I lie down and think to myself, "Jesus, I am in pain today. You also felt this way many times, didn't you? You didn't take any public transportation, but walked the long distances between Judah and Samaria and Galilee! Like me, your feet must have hurt, and your back must have been sore. But, despite all that, you served

---

2 Jane L. Borthwick, ed., "Thy Will Be Done," *Hymns from the Land of Luther* (Edinburgh: W.P. Kennedy, 1854), 58.

us faithfully, didn't you? Please give me strength, Lord, to do my best."

When we endure and share in the same kind of pain that Christ experienced, we learn more about what it means to be one with him.

11

An Image Forever
Burned into the Heart
(Proverbs 24:32–34)

We come at last to the final chapter of the book, where we will conclude our meditations on the book of Proverbs. We have learned much about laziness and diligence in the previous chapters. We have seen that our sinful tendency to be lazy is a result of the fall, and how we were created to labor in love for the glory of God. We also saw how laziness manifests itself even in our ignorance of its danger. In chapters 3 and 4 we discussed the desire for, development of, and carelessness of laziness as a result of self-love, and later we noted how that self-love leads to a hedge of thorns. Next we considered laziness in the context of sleep, observing the importance and purpose of godly rest. In the last two chapters before this one, we saw how laziness intersects with boredom of the soul and how our lethargy grieves the heart of God. In this final chapter, we will examine Proverbs 24:32 to glean our final instruction from this ancient book: "Then I saw and considered it; I looked and received instruction."

An Image Forever Burned into the Heart

If we look at the Hebrew text of Proverbs 24:32, what is noteworthy is the emphasis on looking, where we see two different words—*chazah* and *ra'ah*—each with a distinct nuance but both describing apparently similar actions.

Let us look at the semantics first. When we consider its meaning, *chazah* is more intense than *ra'ah*, for the former refers to the object of observation being ingrained in the heart and mind of the observer, like a picture. The latter refers to a brief observation with the eyes. So the author is referring to the field of a sluggard and the vineyard of a man lacking sense mentioned in the verses previous (Prov 24:30–31):

> I passed by the field of a sluggard,
>   by the vineyard of a man lacking sense,
> and behold, it was all overgrown with thorns;
>   the ground was covered with nettles,
>   and its stone wall was broken down.

He is emphasizing how he will *chazah* this scene—never forgetting it, for the sight has been forever burned into his heart and mind like a picture. Compared to *chazah*, *ra'ah* is innocuous and casual; it refers to no real, lasting effect. So, seeing the abandoned and devastated field and grapevines must have made quite an impression on the author. The fact that he wrote this little narrative from his perspective (note the repetition of the pronoun "I") when it was not necessary to do so reveals his desire to emphasize what he saw and learned.

But was the author of this proverb the only person to have passed by the field and grapevines? Most likely not; many people would have passed by them. While the author was traumatized by the sight and the subtle implications of his observations, most people did not think much of it. Most would have simply passed by nonchalantly, without a second thought, and they would fall into one of the following two categories: (1) people who do not struggle with the issue of carelessness because they are diligent and faithful, and therefore do not think twice about it, and (2) people who are just as lazy and negligent as the owner of the field, and therefore are apathetic about the state of their land and their future well-being. Which type of person would you be?

Examine Yourself with Objective Eyes

Two people can look at the same object yet each come to a different conclusion about what it is. If there are two people looking at this field and these grapevines, one person may be thinking to himself how grateful he is that he is not as lazy as the owner of this field (see Luke 18:9–14), while the other may feel great empathy and pity for the owner, realizing that he himself may be just as lazy as the owner of the field in other areas. Although which reaction we have comes down to what kind of life we have lived up to this point, there is an important factor to consider: Do we honestly know ourselves?

There are many times when our knowledge and ways are very different from those of God and other people (Prov 16:2). Why is this? There could be many reasons, but one of them is the fact that many of us do not examine ourselves objectively (i.e., biblically). There may be people who, after reading this book, think to themselves, "My husband needs to read this book more than I do," or "This is what I have been trying to tell my older brother all this time!" Of course, I am not saying that having those thoughts is wrong, provided they flow from a humble and sympathetic heart. What I am pointing out as wrong is when our first instinct is not to look inward and examine ourselves but to look outward at others as objects to evaluate according to certain standards. Too often, we are wrong about our self-evaluations. We deceive ourselves and are blind to who we really are, thinking that we are better than we actually are.

Let us consider what Jesus told the Laodicean church: "For you say, I am rich, I have prospered, and I need nothing, not realizing that you are wretched, pitiable, poor, blind, and naked" (Rev 3:17). When this verse was written, Laodicea was famous for its treatment of certain eye problems. In the same way that Gaesung is famous for ginseng, Laodicea was famous for eye medicine during the days of the Roman Empire. This is why Laodicea was such an affluent city—it was a city that served a special purpose in the medical field. Because most Laodiceans were so wealthy and financially secure, most of them thought that they did not need anything else. But Jesus thought differently. Jesus confronted their complacency by calling them blind and then telling them to put on some eye medicine (Rev 3:18), the same that they manufactured and sold! This is because they could not see themselves properly. The veil of pride had gotten in the way.

Let us ever remember that there is nothing more dangerous than our ego and pride. Every human has a weakness in common: being too generous and lenient toward our pride. That is why we must make every effort be very strict and examine ourselves by the standard of Scripture. In other words, we must make a habit of looking inward when we read biblical wisdom and character critiques. *We are the ones to whom God is speaking when we read Scripture, not someone else.* If that is the case, we must begin to cultivate godly self-assessment, and leave the assessment of others in God's hands.

Gauging Our Laziness

So how are we to determine whether we are diligent or lazy in the eyes of God? For those who want to avoid any justification of themselves and truly desire an objective answer, I would like to ask a question: When you observe someone being lazy, how do you feel? Are you indifferent? Annoyed? Do you go beyond annoyance to righteous anger? Your answer to this question is re- velatory of your own stance on laziness. But if you are going to ask yourself this question, be warned: you may find that hypocrisy is just around the corner. If it's not, then you will at least be able to get a sense of how you yourself behave. Your reaction to laziness in others can uncover your own values and give you a sense of how lazy you tend to be. This is not a comfortable process to go through, but it is necessary for Christians called to diligence by a self-giving God.

As you attempt to gauge your own laziness and work out your own aspirations for Christlike diligence, it may help to remember that there are two types of diligence: (1) the diligence that is influenced by and given by God and (2) inherent diligence that someone is simply born with as a mark of his or her personality. With the latter, if there is no synergistic balance between the soul and flesh, people act faithfully and diligently simply for the sake of their happiness or because it seems natural to them—and perhaps they do not know why. But the latter kind of diligence is not the sort that results from being broken.

Let me give you an example. My father is a very diligent person. He has advanced in years and is not the same as he used to be, but I have yet to see him sleep past four thirty in the morning— even before he was saved and received grace. Whenever I would get out of bed to go to early-morning prayer, he was already up and listening to the radio. I do not know how he was able to wake up so early and do all that he did, but it seems as if he was able to do so because he was born with diligence; it was not something that he developed through his faith or by God's explicit influence through special revelation.

The first kind of diligence—the kind that is given and shaped by God—works a change in us. After having been influenced by God, a person who makes the effort to live diligently will feel righteous anger when observing someone's laziness—not a judgmental self-righteousness but a holy, God-centered anger. This is an appropriate and preferred response and emotion for Christians because the person who lives lazily is wasting not merely his own time and effort, but also God's time and effort. In addition, such a person is tarnishing the name of God rather than bringing it glory, and that is what all people (Christian and non-Christian) were designed to do.

This idea can be hard for some of us to accept. Can we really have a sense of righteous anger without our ego or pride becoming inflated in the process? Yes, but only because this is a work of God's Spirit; it is not our doing. And once God works this change in us by his Spirit, we begin to see the world in a whole new light. Everything that we do then becomes a battlefield: a patch of life that will be claimed either by the sinful self or the regenerate self. The former gives insult to God; the latter brings him glory. So the domain of laziness is not limited to merely the issues of getting the amount of sleep that one desires, or abandoning one's duties. These are just the most noticeable. *Any attempt at trying to reap big harvests with very little work by cutting corners and using unethical methods is laziness in God's eyes.* Therefore, it is perfectly natural and proper for anyone living for God's glory—wrestling with issues of sin and holiness, gifted with the passion to persevere—to be absolutely disgusted at the lifestyle and choices of the lazy. This does not make these people better than others; it simply shows that they have been changed so dramatically that their sensitivity to sin has increased. They see in the world all that was already there, but now they *truly* see it, and it grieves them, just as it grieves God.

This is a matter of Spirit-wrought faith, a passionate faith, and the contrast to it is easy to spot. When people who did not attend

Sunday service are asked why did they not attend, most of them respond as if they were dead. They nonchalantly mutter an excuse: they were too busy with work; they had to deal with a cutthroat environment at their company; their bodies were in pain or hurting. Every single one of these issues is difficult, and all of them may be true and legitimate reasons for not attending worship. However, we must be candid with ourselves and earnestly live by faith, knowing that Satan loves nothing more than to toss an obstacle in our way on Sunday morning. Isn't this true especially in these days, when there are many trials, fears, and numerous temptations facing all of us? Considering this context, faith is what prevents us from walking hand in hand with our laziness and drifting far away from God. Faith binds us to diligence just as it binds us to the risen Christ.

Discerning and Applying Is More Important Than Our Amount of Experience

Let us return to Proverbs 24:32. The author of this proverb received instruction when he laid his eyes on the lazy and foolish man's farmland, covered with weeds and briars. Although he learned something practical through his observation, the best thing about all of this is the fact that there was a personal experience connected to the lesson. The author of Proverbs had a firsthand experience on which to meditate. This is not always the case for us (in fact, it's rarely the case for us). Sometimes it can be quite costly to learn something through a direct experience, or we might be kept from learning something because of our pride. That is why we have

God's Word: we receive instruction from God's Word concerning these things.

This does not mean there is no value in imagining what the author originally experienced. When we consider the laziness depicted in this passage, there is a helpful way to realize how evil it really is: we can imagine looking at the field as if it were our own. By imagining this, we will be devastated at the thought of our own sin—we all have our sinful fields of briars—and we will come to realize just how much grief, suffering, and agony laziness brings to us and to God.

At the same time, it is foolish to try to personally experience anything about which the Bible has already given a definitive conclusion. Whereas an unwise person begins taking a bottle of dangerous medicine and tilts his head back to finish the entire bottle for the sake of experience, and then dies, a wise person may take a sip and stop there instead of trying to finish the bottle. The wise person learns from what he experiences and lets that knowledge guide his decisions. The fool lives as if he must prove everything through experience and fails to take into account clearly revealed truth.

Passages such as Proverbs 24:32 do not present these images simply to tell us to look at them and learn, but to warn us against making the same mistakes. The very wise thing that the author of this proverb did was to show concern and respond in his own life to the actions of the sluggard, even if the sluggard's behavior did not exactly match his own.

As we already mentioned, the author of this proverb was King Solomon. Because he was king, Solomon normally would not have had the time to go to the field or the vineyard and help revive it.

But he would have attained much actual knowledge about his attitude and posture toward life through his time observing the field and vineyard, and we can learn from his insightful observation.

Of course, we are very different from Solomon. If you and I did not have to worry about where our next meal was going to come from, we would still not be like this ancient king, and that is OK. We are nevertheless similar to him. What's more, to our shame, we are similar to the man who let his field and vineyard go untended. The field and vineyard that appear in Proverbs 24:30–31, therefore, are not just someone else's. Those are *our* field and vineyard, too. Don't we all have moments when, instead of shedding much blood, sweat, and tears at our daily work in order to produce an abundant yield, we allow weeds and thorns to fill our fields because of our laziness? The longer we continue to live like this and to consider it a small matter, the shorter is our time to truly live for God. Seconds and minutes show no partiality to the diligent person or the lazy person. We are all moving forward toward eternity, and we are never able to gain back what we lose to lethargy.

A Goose That Lays Golden Eggs

Throughout this book, I hope I have made it plain that our relationship with God is the root of our lives, and laziness tries to eat away at that; it tries to corrode the foundation of our spiritual and physical well-being. The carnal desires of the flesh that follow after the desires of laziness help in the task of eating away at the true root of our lives. Laziness is a slow and silent spiritual assassin, and we must ever be vigilant against it.

Perhaps an old story will help to clarify our condition. Many people are familiar with the story of the goose that laid golden eggs. The goose laid one golden egg every day, but its owner became greedy and wanted more than one at a time. Therefore, he killed the goose in the hope of finding a stash of golden eggs inside it. In the end, his greed left him without anything and caused him to kill the source of his treasure.

Whenever I see Christians so "busy" (busy for self, but lazy for God) that they have no time left to invest in their relationship with God, I think about the owner of the goose. No matter how greedy one may be or how desperate one's situation is, one thing that should never be replaced is our devotional life with God. When we harvest lettuce from our fields, we do so by cutting off the leaves only and not the roots. Otherwise, the crop will not grow again for the following harvest. It is the same with our spiritual lives. If it is true that our relationship with God is the root of our lives, then the time that we devote to praying and to reading and meditating on his Word is invaluable, and we must guard that time from anything else that might invade or take over. The moment that a believer decides to replace that precious time with God and his Word with a focus on worldly success or personal greed is the moment that he becomes the owner who killed his golden goose. We cannot cut open a hidden source of blessings and take them all as we please. We receive as the Lord gives, and the Lord always gives when his creatures prayerfully meditate on his Word.

Mark this: the Christians who suffer most in this world are those who are too busy with everything worldly and do not spend any time with God. In doing this, they lose the resources of heaven and forget their Creator. They might be rich in the world's eyes, but in God's eyes they are destitute, for they have forgotten the grace of Jesus Christ that has restrained their egos. They have traded eternal riches for temporal ones. For Christians who find themselves in this position, imagine what it would be like if God took a leave of absence, if he suspended his grace and patience for a day. In such a dark world (for God is our light), they would become slaves.

When Boredom and Laziness Hold Hands

Sometimes, we do not experience any progress and growth in our holiness—even if we work tirelessly for it. Sometimes God is testing our patience and purifying our faith in the present circumstances. Other times, we fail to experience progress because we have not surrendered our love for sin (that is, we retain self-love). If we continue to live this way, we will live in constant conflict, and nothing will get better. In fact, things might actually get worse, because this struggle will cause our souls to be disgusted and sick of everything, which will then lead us to fall into laziness.

When this utter boredom of the soul and laziness of the flesh come together and join hands, every good goal related to one's faith disappears. We become blinded to God's greatness, and we even forget how to bring him glory in what we do.

Imagine someone who is drowning in the waters of sin because he is strapped to luggage that contains his worldly passions. Even if this person wanted to come out of the water and stand on the rock of Christ, the luggage that he is wearing would prevent him from ever being able to get out. Yet he refuses to throw the bags off his shoulder because he believes that they are filled to the brim with gold. As his indecisiveness prolongs his fighting within himself, the limits of his strength are exhausted in the water. He is not able to swim to safety while second-guessing whether it is worth it to put up such a strong effort to not sink. It is in this moment that his laziness becomes like a large millstone hanging around his neck. He is no longer able to put up a legitimate resistance and stay afloat, and soon he is sinking slowly into the waters of sin.

It follows, then, that we must be vigilant and stand fast the moment we feel our souls reaching for the baggage of this world. If we believe that the work we are doing is right in God's eyes, that cannot lead us to become lackadaisical. We must pray that God continues to give us the passion to do our work for his glory. If we do not serve and fulfill our duties with any passion, a rebellious spirit will burrow its way into our hearts and begin to grow stronger, feeding on the lifeblood of our indwelling sin.

To guard against that rebellious spirit, we must say "amen" when we feel convicted of our own laziness, and then work diligently to remedy it with the Spirit's guidance. A true and genuine "amen" does not come from our lips, but from our lives. Whether we have heard a sermon or understood a biblical truth in a fresh way, the "amen" must come through our decisive action to do all for the glory of God. Vigilance, I have said all along, is critical.

The Danger of Sleeping Just a Little Longer

Notice how the author of Proverbs was able to learn a valuable lesson that will stick with him for a while just by seeing the field and the grapevines of the sluggard. That lesson is this: if humans are easily swayed to sleep more, to be more sluggish, and to lie down for just a little longer, this can quickly turn into a path toward our destruction. Of course, some of you may be thinking to yourselves, "So it's a sin to sleep, to be weary, or to lie down?" Certainly not! These things are not sins. It is not the *matter* of our actions that we have in mind here; it is the *motive*. The real problem is when those things become habitual issues that grow out of our self-love. When the motive is foul, the soul will go awry. It follows that when we are warned by our conscience, we tend to stop asking whether doing it is a sin or not. Instead, we begin to ask how far we can go without crossing the line.

As we have seen in this passage from Proverbs and in several others, sleeping, being sluggish, and lying down for just a little longer easily results in poverty and want. Remember that laziness is like the thief in the lazy farmer's field: it robs us and conquers us without our lifting a limb. This, once more, is not a call to self-persecution and self-abuse. It is merely biblical advice to be dedicated to our duties. All of us humans must lie down and sleep when we grow weary; rest is not a sin. The problem is not in the action itself, but in the motive behind it. Having a selfish motive can easily lead to the abuse of what God has designed to be good.

Now, I am well aware that it takes tremendous effort for us to be precisely aware of what God requires of us each day, and to have the enthusiasm to give it our all. Having a heart that earnestly seeks God's glory by fulfilling what he has given us to do is not so common. It never has been, and it probably never will be. But that is no reason to cease striving for such a heart and asking for it repeatedly in prayer. We cannot resolve to wait for God to do things *for* us when he has always chosen to do things *through* us.

Tasting the Essence of Faith through Application

A diligent life and spiritual well-being are integrally related. When someone sets goals for God's glory and then faithfully lives them out, brokenness is abundant in him, for to get to the point of achieving goals for the glory of God one *must* be broken. Glorifying God comes only after we have died to ourselves. We must care nothing for our own pride or image and focus entirely on God's greatness. So, if we find ourselves asking the question, "If I don't see the results I want to even though I gave it my all, won't God be disappointed in me?"—this is a clear sign that we have not wholly surrendered to God's will. When we do surrender fully to God and give our all for his glory, we will be freed from anxiety and concern—regardless of the outcome. Whether we succeed or fail in the world's eyes, we will be grateful for having been given the opportunity to love and honor the one who gave himself for us. Being this committed, of course, requires continual self-assessment. All of us are bound to hit walls in our attempts to work for God's glory. It is during these moments that we must humble ourselves and begin to pray more, leaning trustfully upon God. And we do not depart from God's presence when we succeed, either. When we complete the work that God has given us, then we can praise him for the grace he has given us to do what he required. God is *all* for the diligent person.

If we do not devote ourselves to our work, a burden will remain on our hearts regardless of our success or failure. When all is well, we tend to become prideful; when it is not, we complain. The only way to avoid these experiences is to give ourselves wholly to his service. It is only then that we will be able to leave behind worldly anguish and regret, for God will use all his servant's labor for his own purposes. Instead of being seized by great regret, continuously beating our chests and thinking to ourselves, "Why did I do that?" we can rest in knowing that our labor is not in vain if it is labor for the Lord (1 Cor 15:58).

It is here, at the end of this book, that we are coming to the essence of Christian faith: the place where biblical belief meets godly practice. *The essence of the Christian faith is known and experienced through the application of one's faith.* While loving God, spending time in prayer and in the Word, and learning to walk on the road of sanctification are all crucial, the essence of faith is not simply something to be known through study; it is experienced through the struggle of chasing after the truth. The essence of love is experienced in a life that deeply loves God, and the essence of prayer is experienced in a place where prayer is frequently practiced.

Laziness, of course, prevents any of this from ever happening, and prevents the believer from ever experiencing the essence of true faith. As an artificial satellite revolves around the earth continuously but never actually touches the earth, so it is with laziness and our faith. We may get close to real faith but never touch the surface of it because of the barrier of laziness, which keeps us in orbit around our sinful selves.

Now, I know many people read books on prayer in order to grow in their ability to pray, or they invite speakers who are great evangelizers to their churches in order to hold seminars on evangelism so that they might better practice it, or they listen to lectures on holiness in order to become more holy, or they even listen to the testimonies of those who are faithful in an attempt to become more faithful themselves. But this is not living by faith, it is admiring the faith of others. Faith grows in depth only as it is lived out in breadth. When we do not practice what is revealed to us in God's Word, we abandon not only our God-given duties but also our spiritual well-being and livelihood.

Pour Yourself Out for Your Calling

As we noted at the outset, the life of diligence is not a life of isolation. We live most faithfully when we are surrounded by the body of Christ, so we should seek the counsel and advice of others to see what they believe our duties are, and whether we are being faithful in what God has entrusted to us already. If we have not been faithful, we need to repent and seek out new ways to give God our all. Our time, our resources, our passions—all of these things must be oriented to the triune God of Scripture, spent in the service of his glory.

We use our time to write a letter to God—a very long letter confessing our love for him. We do not write letters to ourselves; our time is not our own. If we live our lives without God-centered goals and waste our time by living lazily, we rob God of the words we might put in our letter. And we have every reason to write all of our lives into this letter. Just consider the precious gifts that God has given us—our families, homes, schools, and jobs! Every detail in our daily lives points to the grace of God, who lavished his riches upon us in countless ways. And this God went beyond all that we could hope or imagine and gave us his own Son! Do we have any reason to be reluctant by giving God less than all of our lives?

I Am Happy to Be Living for God

Think about the two thieves who were crucified alongside Jesus. One thief went to hell, and the other thief went to paradise with Christ. The thief who repented may have been someone who lived his entire life for himself, doing hardly anything good for God. But in his last moments, he recognized that Jesus was the Son of God, repented of his sins, and received mercy. He realized who Jesus was, and after thinking about the life that he had lived, he could not bring himself to ask Jesus to save him. That is why he asked, "Jesus, remember me when you come into your kingdom" (Luke 23:42). But Jesus looked on him and accepted his faith, and saved him. He gladly made him a companion on the road to heaven.

Let us think about this thief for a moment. Jesus had much love for him; with joy, he was able to bring this thief along with him to heaven. But what was the thief feeling and thinking at the time? After living a life in sin, for the first time he had someone to serve and knew how he had to live. But, unfortunately, his life would come to an end that day on the cross. How agonizing and frustrating it must have been for him—to know his Lord and yet not have any time left to serve him! After a life of darkness, he found light. He finally had a renewed purpose, knew whom he had to serve, and had a heart to serve, but had no more time to do so. If he were given some time to serve the Lord in whatever capacity, he would have been overjoyed. Perhaps he would have sought out other criminals in order to share the love of Christ and call them to repentance. He might also have served the Lord by sharing the gospel and the love of Christ with his surviving family members. But he was never given that chance.

When we compare ourselves to this thief, we are so blessed and fortunate to have many opportunities and chances to serve the Lord. The Lord gladly receives our service, and walks with us during our journey to heaven.

Let us live our lives faithfully, waging spiritual warfare against our laziness, and striving to live passionately and diligently every day for the Lord of glory. One day, we will exchange our spiritual combat gear for a fine linen garment. The question for all of us is, Will we feel regret in handing over a military uniform that was barely used? Can we learn from a thief who lived two thousand years ago and start pouring ourselves out for Christ today?

ABOUT THE AUTHOR

Rev. Nam Joon Kim is Senior Pastor of Yullin Church (GAPC) in Pyeongchon, South Korea. He holds master's degrees in divinity and theology from Chongshin University, and served as a lecturer and assistant professor at An-Yang University and Chon-An University. He is the author of numerous books and articles in Korean.